RUNAWAY GROWTH

Ford,

Keep taking one more step and keep inspiring

RUNAWAY GROWTH

Seven Life and Business Lessons
from Running Marathons
across Seven Continents

Satish Shenoy

NEW DEGREE PRESS

COPYRIGHT © 2022 SATISH SHENOY

All rights reserved.

RUNAWAY GROWTH

Seven Life and Business Lessons from Running Marathons across Seven Continents

ISBN

979-8-88504-139-3   *Paperback*
979-8-88504-772-2   *Kindle Ebook*
979-8-88504-251-2   *Digital Ebook*

This book is dedicated to
My parents Sadananda and Sudha Shenoy
for being a constant source of inspiration,
for their sacrifice for the greater good,
and, for their wisdom and generosity.

My wife, Deepa, and our children,
Snigdha and Sandeep Shenoy
for being my rock, my heart, and my soul.

You, who can achieve impossible goals.

CONTENTS

PART 1	**WHAT GOT YOU HERE WON'T GET YOU THERE**	**11**
CHAPTER 1	INTRODUCTION: THE MIRAGE OF THE IMPOSSIBLE	13
CHAPTER 2	SMALL GOALS, BIG DREAMS	29
CHAPTER 3	REACHING HIGHER	43
CHAPTER 4	SHOWING UP	53
PART 2	**THE PRINCIPLES**	**61**
CHAPTER 5	MINDSET	63
CHAPTER 6	IT TAKES A VILLAGE	75
CHAPTER 7	PREPARATION	93
CHAPTER 8	GRIT	113
CHAPTER 9	PROGRESS	131
CHAPTER 10	AUDACITY	141
CHAPTER 11	FINISHING STRONG	151
PART 3	**APPLYING THE PRINCIPLES**	**161**
CHAPTER 12	AFTERWORD	163
CHAPTER 13	A COLLECTION OF KEY REFLECTIONS	165
CHAPTER 14	THE SEVEN-CONTINENT ADVENTURE: A PHOTO JOURNEY	179
	ACKNOWLEDGMENTS	197
	APPENDIX	205

*So many of our dreams first seem impossible,
then they seem improbable,
and then when we summon the will,
they soon become inevitable.*

—CHRISTOPHER REEVE

PART 1

WHAT GOT YOU HERE WON'T GET YOU THERE

CHAPTER 1

INTRODUCTION: THE MIRAGE OF THE IMPOSSIBLE

"Impossible is not a fact. It is an opinion. It is not a declaration. It is a dare. Impossible is temporary. It is nothing!"

—MUHAMMAD ALI

It was January 8, 2012—a crisp, cold Californian winter morning.

The warmth and the caffeine from the hot chai I had gulped down had not quite kicked in. As I drove to Campbell Park, the frigid morning air sent shivers down my spine, waking me by the time I arrived. *Whose idea was this? What on earth prompted me to leave the cocoon of my warm bed?*

Often, when we embark on an ambitious project or undertaking, it is normal to feel a blanket of fog or resentment settle around us. Our intended destination may be clear, but the details and the process of getting to that destination are much less so. One part of us may be eternally optimistic, while the other part may be weighed down by fears, uncertainties, and doubts.

As I started my own journey that January morning, one thing was clear: My ultimate goal was to run a full marathon. All 26.2 miles of it. How and when I would fulfill that goal was unclear. But I had promised myself two things: that I had to try and that I had to get started. Even if that start was going to be small.

The initial practice runs, which were only a handful of miles and "small" by marathon standards, felt formidable and uncomfortable to me as a relatively novice runner. And the goal of completing a full marathon felt improbable, if not impossible. If you had told me then of the fabulous twists and turns, the ups and downs in my adventure ahead, I would not have believed you. If you had said my running shoes were also made for flying all over the world, I would have called you irrationally exuberant. In the end, my journey felt much like Walter's journey in the movie *The Adventures of Walter Mitty* played brilliantly by Ben Stiller (Stiller, 2013)—a journey that, at times, was filled with happiness, euphoria, and adventure, and, at other times, filled with anxiety, pain, and disappointment. In the end, something told me that I was going to learn and grow from this journey. And the adventure was out there waiting for me.

Looking back, I have realized the goals that seemed so intimidating when I started this journey were only an illusion. For those of you who have taken a road trip, you will relate to this quick story. It is a hot, sunny day and you are driving down the road for what seems like an eternity. You look on the horizon and see a mirage on the hot tarmac ahead. As you drive farther and approach the spot where you thought you saw something shiny, that mirage disappears. But then, the next one appears on the horizon. There it is again in the distance. As you get closer to that next spot where you conjured up that figment of imagination, it disappears once more. A big goal that feels unreachable is like that mirage.

My first illusion was that running a marathon was improbable, or even impossible. Once I crossed the finish line of my first marathon, I was able to dispel that. My next illusion was that running marathons across more than one continent was challenging. I dismissed that too very quickly. And then a bigger illusion came up on the horizon: that running marathons across all seven continents was impossible. Even a little crazy. Soon, I was also able to destroy that mirage. Over time, I was able to tackle every one of those mirages that appeared on my way to fulfilling the dream of running marathons across all seven continents. This journey was not without its challenges and obstacles—far from it. This book is the story of that unlikely journey and what I have learned from my experience, the experiences of others like me, and how you can apply those learnings to sports, business, or life.

If you are like most people involved in any kind of sport, a major project at work, or your first venture, you are also striving hard to get incrementally closer to your goal, even if that goal seems daunting or impossible at first.

Back at Campbell Park, as I parked my car, the boisterous group of people who had congregated near the basketball courts came into view, which was otherwise devoid of people this early in the morning. I watched from my warm car as the group was getting ready, talking loudly while jogging in place, the steam coming out of their noses and mouths, vaporizing the frozen air, and making them look like incessant smokers. Every few minutes, a new person joined this group, laughing, hugging energetically, and exchanging high-fives all around. As hard as it was for me to leave the warmth of the car, I braced myself before getting ready to join the others. As I alighted, a familiar face from within the group—my relative Shankar—waved energetically, trying to get my attention and motioning me to come over.

I walked over to where Shankar was vigorously stretching, and the haze of what had prompted all of this began to lift.

It was December 2011, and I had been invited to several year-end parties. Often, at those parties, we seemed to reflect on the year that had been and celebrate the new beginning arriving on our doorstep. At one of those parties, a small group of us were discussing the preferred means to get rid of all the excess guilt and the extra pounds of those rich meals we were gorging on throughout the holidays. Running, hiking, biking, badminton, basketball, and even gardening were fair game; a robust conversation ensued. One of my acquaintances in the group mentioned she had recently taken up running and she had better luck sticking to it after she started running with a group. Others in the group mentioned hiking as an alternative as it was better on the knees, especially as we all got older. We all had a good laugh about the realities of aging and its impact on the body.

After some playful banter about who was doing the most intense fitness activity, I expressed that I wanted to try running a marathon. My own rationale was that running didn't need any extra equipment; it felt like meditation (in motion), and you could stop anytime you wanted.

An experienced runner at the party, with a plate full of food and a mouth full of alcohol and sarcasm, remarked that running was not for everyone. "After all, it would be harder for people on the heavier side," he chuckled, smirking, while glancing at the few extra pounds I had lugged around my gut for years. Carrying on with his cynicism, he made a most audacious prediction. "Running a marathon is impossible for most," he barked.

While I was a tad overweight, it had never occurred to me that running a marathon was "impossible" per se. Or even beyond my limits. Just for a moment, I doubted myself. This exchange reminded me of one of my favorite quotes from a famous Irish playwright and critic.

> "The reasonable man adapts himself to the world; the unreasonable one persists in trying to adapt the world to himself. Therefore, all progress depends on the unreasonable man."
>
> —GEORGE BERNARD SHAW.

Is it reasonable for me to aspire to run a marathon? Time to be unreasonable and challenge myself, I thought.

A few seconds later, the boisterous laughter around me brought me back to my senses. All eyes of the group were still on me, waiting for a response.

"I will never know until I try, will I?" was all I could muster.

An awkward silence followed. The group moved on to the next topic, but my mind was still stuck on that prior conversation and particularly on the comment that I felt was directed at me. Although I had done a fair bit of hiking and rock climbing during my time in Colorado a few years ago, running was never my "thing." It was not something I enjoyed in my younger years in school, college, or even while hiking the gorgeous mountains of Colorado. I resolved that I would give running a shot.

As luck would have it, Shankar and his wife (my cousin, Anandi), had invited me and my family over to their place for dinner later that week. While enjoying a wonderful dinner, Shankar told me that he had taken up running and doing that with a group had made it much easier for him. That sounded familiar; I had heard something similar from the lady at the other party earlier in the week. I was over the moon to hear this again as it reinforced the idea that perhaps that is what I needed to do. When I mentioned to Shankar that the idea of running with the group intrigued me, he invited me right away to join him and his group the next morning. I felt like I had just won the lottery.

That day in Campbell Park, I ran two miles with the group, and I struggled. The saving grace was that after two to three minutes of running, we slowed down and started walking. Before I realized why we had stopped running and started walking, one of our mentors, Krishnan, explained that we were doing the "run/

walk/run method," or "interval running." "We will run part of the time and walk part of the time. And these timeframes are called 'intervals,'" Krishnan explained. "This will let you break into running without too much exertion and also reduce the likelihood of injuries." I later found out that this running technique was invented and popularized by one of my running idols whom I had hoped to meet someday, Jeff Galloway, in his book *The Run-Walk-Run Method* (Galloway, 2016).

Leveraging this technique, we would *run* for about two minutes and then *walk* for two minutes, or a run-to-walk ratio of two-to-two (i.e., 2:2) as is known by seasoned runners. As we got more experience under our belts, Krishnan added that we could run more and walk less during the intervals, i.e., three-to-one or four-to-one (i.e., 3:1 or 4:1). But that would have to wait for a few weeks, or even months. I will admit that initially, even two-to-one felt challenging! But then, seeing everyone else going through the same struggles comforted me that I was not alone. "No runner left behind" was our motto. We turned around at the mile-one mark to the relief of most of us rookie runners. We kept up with the two-to-one interval, and the end of mile two was now in sight.

As we approached our finishing point, I felt a bit of a high. *Maybe it was the chai finally kicking in!* I thought. But something told me it was more than that. It was the high from having successfully crossed my first milestone. After we were done running and we were stretching for a few minutes, Krishnan reminded us of the weekday running schedule he had shared earlier and directed us to ask the assigned mentors if we had questions. We all agreed we would. As I was getting back into the car to drive home, a question popped into my head: Is running *for me?* A strong "maybe" was the answer.

On Tuesday night, Krishnan, my assigned mentor, called me. "How are you doing?" he asked. When I told him I was a bit sore from running, he said, "Well, that was to be expected. You know how to get rid of it?" he inquired.

"Maybe more stretching?" I replied, tentatively.

"No!" he laughed. "More running."

So, during the week, we continued running for at least three days, and then four days a week as our muscles got used to running. We would run distances of various lengths that gradually increased over a four-month period, from a couple of miles to a dozen miles. Initially, all of us new runners struggled a lot. The discipline, the commitment, the endurance was a tall ask. But then, it was amazing to see how all those asks seemed less onerous when you saw your peers step up and your coaches and mentors made it look easy.

The following weekend, it was time for my next long run. We had to get beyond the two miles that we had *conquered* the prior weekend. We attempted three miles. Although I was concerned about whether I could run three miles, my peers seemed to accept the challenge, even though they probably all had their doubts; this is the magic of groupthink, or "herd mentality" as it is better known. We accomplished our goal that day, even though it seemed to be a struggle. It did feel a tad better than the prior weekend's run, though. Over the next four months, we continued to increase our running mileage gradually (both with the weekday runs and weekend long runs) and got all the way up to twenty-four miles of long runs. If you had asked me when I started running if I would ever see the day when I would run twenty-four miles at a stretch, I would have thought you were out of your mind or simply laughed at the idea.

Keep in mind that this didn't happen overnight. Every three to four weeks, on our weekend long runs, we would back down to the prior weekend's goal. For example, a sequence of weekend long runs would look like this:

- First weekend: two miles
- Second weekend: four miles
- Third weekend: six miles
- Fourth weekend: eight miles
- Fifth weekend: six miles
- Sixth weekend: ten miles
- Seventh weekend: twelve miles
- Eighth weekend: fourteen miles
- Ninth weekend: twelve miles
- Tenth weekend: sixteen miles
- and so on...

This approached helped us take a break, both mentally and physically, and enabled us to keep increasing miles over time, while also avoiding injuries. I could hardly believe that so many miles were in me! Sometimes I was very sore, especially when I got beyond the eight-to-ten-mile mark, and I even doubted my ability to keep up with the increasing miles. But my mind was made, and my body seemed to listen. Running with a group and seeing others step up to the challenge bolstered my own self-belief.

Like a marathon in running, a great example of a "marathon" in business would be to launch a startup as an entrepreneur or attempt a "moonshot" project at work.

I once heard this inspiring quote on entrepreneurship…

"The magic of entrepreneurship is the idea of wanting to take the impossible and make it real."

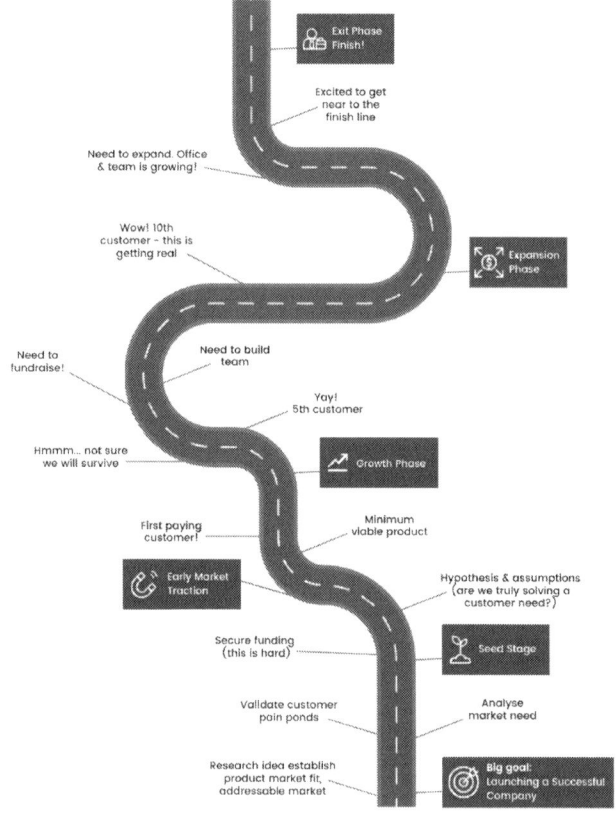

A Startup Founder's "Marathon" Journey

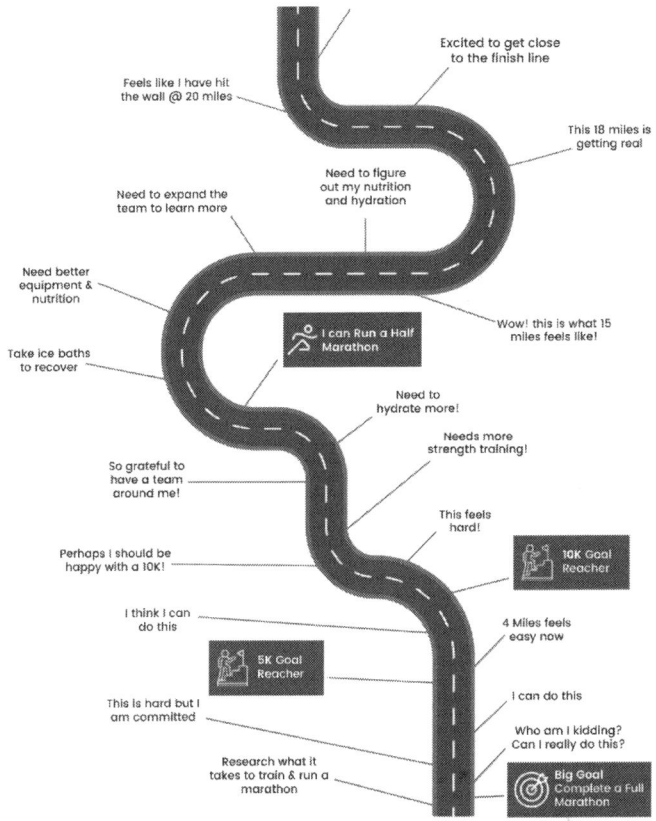

A Runner's Marathon Journey

Having worked for both early and late-stage startups in my career, I can relate to the "marathon" journey of launching a startup.

Startup founders need at least one big idea (of course, multiple ideas help!), and that big idea is broken down into a set of smaller yet progressively harder goals they need to complete to successfully execute their big idea. They need a great team around them to succeed. They need to build a plan and implement that consistently over years to have their idea see the light of the day. Like a marathoner, they will need to incorporate "short runs" (short projects or sprints) and "long runs" (longer projects or the dreaded "all-nighters" to get something critical done!). They will continue to build the team, raise funding, and grow the startup. As most marathon runners do, they will invariably have many triumphs, struggles, disappointments, and lessons learned along the way. They might hit "the wall" at some point in their startup marathon. (The "wall" is described by most marathon runners as the point at which they feel that they cannot carry on and their body is screaming at them to stop!) The startup founder may overcome "the wall" and any other remaining obstacles and still make it to the finish line—or they may need to pivot and do something else. A "half marathon" analogy is appropriate here, i.e., to take a step back and attempt something smaller before attempting a "full marathon" (i.e., their big idea) again. Ultimately, it is their own "marathon" to run.

Now, let's talk about you. Perhaps you are dreaming of taking your idea and launching your own startup. Perchance, you want to run—just around the block? A 5K? A 10K? A marathon or many marathons? Across one state or all fifty states? Across one continent or all seven continents? Maybe you want to write a book. Or you have been looking for a more exciting job than the one you currently have!

Are you feeling that some of those goals or aspirations are hard to reach or are even impossible? Are they really, or is that notion that your goal is impossible a mirage? Have you given up at any point or even *thought* of giving up? If so, welcome to the club. You need to be unreasonable, like George Bernard Shaw said.

WHY I WROTE THIS BOOK

My big dream of completing marathons across the seven continents was an unlikely one, when I first had that dream, almost a decade ago. Through the guidance of mentors and coaches and through experimentation, I learned some great lessons and principles along the way. In time, I was able to ultimately get across that finish line. With your big dream, if you are still in the mindset that some of your big goals are impossible or you have an ounce of doubt in your ability to accomplish those goals, I wrote this book for you.

I hope this book inspires you to achieve more than you previously thought possible. I hope it invigorates you to run your own "marathon"—whether that "marathon" is in running, a challenging or "moonshot" project at work, an entrepreneurial adventure, or something else.

HOW THIS BOOK IS ORGANIZED

This book is organized into three sections:

- Part 1 is the "**What Got You Here Won't Get You There**" section much like preparing for the "marathon," where I will share some of the fundamentals. These fundamentals include how to translate your big dream into small, incremental yet progressively harder goals, how to reach higher, and what it means to show up and how to show up.

- Part 2 is the "core" of the book much like the core muscles your body needs to perform well during a marathon; this part has "**The Principles**." While many aspects helped me throughout my journey, the seven core principles are the ones I truly feel made all the difference and helped me get across that finish line.

- Part 3 is about "**Applying the Principles**," essentially my approach to help you with practical ways to use the principles I shared in Part 2. Think of this as your training plan. At the end of each chapter in Part 1 and 2, I have included a "Key Reflections" section; this is to start getting you to think about applying everything you learn in each chapter. And then, I bring it all together again in one place at the end of Part 3 and call it "A Collection of Key Reflections." We all know a picture is worth a thousand words. So, I decided to share more details of my journey through a photo album I curated for you. Hope you enjoy it.

Many have asked me for my secret in successfully running marathons across all seven continents. While there is no one secret, we will examine some of the behaviors that drive those self-limiting beliefs and how to overcome them. I will share what has helped me and others like me go from "impossible" to "I'm possible." And I know I would enjoy the opportunity to teach you how to apply those principles in your own life—to running, to your work, and to your life.

That is my promise to you.

ONLINE RESOURCES
For an additional set of resources, including free downloads of practical tools, intriguing insights, inspiring quotes,

interesting pictures of my journey, and more, please join me online at https://satishshenoy.com/author/ or scan this QR code to be taken directly to my page:

CHAPTER 2

SMALL GOALS, BIG DREAMS

"Do one thing every day that scares you."

—ELEANOR ROOSEVELT

In her seminal book, *Grit: The Power of Passion and Perseverance*, Dr. Angela Duckworth shares some great insights from a renowned Harvard psychologist, Dr. William James, to further illustrate the importance of getting out of your comfort zone.

In 1907, Dr. James wanted to answer two questions: (1) How is every person's approach in the pursuit of goals uniquely different, and (2) why do most of us do much less than we are capable of?

After a long and distinguished career of understanding and documenting the responses to those questions, Dr. James reflected on his own achievements and failures and those of his closest friends and relatives, and remarked,

> *"Compared to where we ought to be, we are only half-awake. Our fires are dampened. Our drafts are checked. We are making use of only a small part of our mental and physical resources. The human individual usually lives far within his limits; he possesses powers of various sorts, which he habitually fails to use. He energizes below his maximum, and he behaves below his optimum."*

As I mentioned in the prior chapter, when I first started running, I felt that the goal of running a full marathon was quite intimidating. *Twenty-six miles of running…at one time?* I remember asking myself. I had barely run a few miles at one time in my entire life. Clearly, I was helping reinforce Dr. James's prophecies. But over time, I spoke to a few people, gave it further thought, and met some highly accomplished runners and learned from their experiences. I noticed my mindset began to change. As we will discuss in an upcoming chapter, one of the most important aspects of accomplishing your dreams is this changing of your mindset.

In this chapter, we will deal with how to achieve those dreams. What I have found to be a great starting place to fulfilling those goals is to start with smaller goals and then set progressively bigger milestones that get harder over time. Then, as you successfully accomplish the smaller goals, you can easily build on that success. Your confidence grows, and you achieve the next slightly bigger goal. Rinse and repeat.

As you begin to pursue larger goals, you will soon be on the doorstep of fulfilling your big dream. Aiming for goals that are too easy won't keep you motivated, and focusing on goals far beyond your reach will only result in failure and frustration. Either approach will eat away at your sense of competence, which is a basic need to sustain your drive toward a big goal.

Remember Martin Luther King Jr.'s "I have a dream" speech? You bet it was a big dream! And Dr. King showed us that those big dreams can have meaningful outcomes when implemented by setting achievable, smaller goals and relentless execution. Some great examples of Dr. King's efforts may further illustrate this approach.

Dr. King was at the center of the civil rights struggle for over thirteen years. He started with a series of nonviolent protests against discrimination. He tackled the racial challenges in Birmingham by forming the "Birmingham Campaign," for which he recruited members of all ages to join. With the Rosa Parks incident in Montgomery, Dr. King organized the Montgomery Bus Boycott. He then went on to set up the Southern Christian Leadership Conference that led to protests calling for equal voting rights for African Americans. Later, he participated in the Black sanitation workers strike in Memphis. As Dr. King showed us, the best way to accomplish a big dream is to set progressively challenging goals, achieve those goals, and build on that success to fulfill the big dream (World History Edu., 2019).

Some of Dr. King's marquee achievements that are directly or indirectly attributed to his efforts include the passage of the landmark Civil Rights Act of 1964 that dealt with discrimination in schools, employment, and accommodations across America. It guaranteed fairness to all Americans, irrespective of their race, religion, or national affiliation. The Voting Rights Act of 1965 ensured that all sound citizens could exercise their right to vote during major elections. The Fair Housing Act of 1968 abolished discrimination in the rental or sales of houses. Dr. King's big dream, legacy, and achievements are truly one for the ages.

One of the best quotes that I heard with respect to dreaming big was:

> *"Don't just plant a tree; plant an orchard. What you plant in life is also what you harvest."*

So go ahead and dream big.

When we are young, we are asked, "What do you want to become when you grow up?" Most kids will say something spectacular. But somewhere along the way, that dream meets reality and starts to get smaller or even completely disappears. If you are like me and you lost your dream somewhere along the way, now is the time to pick it back up. You may ask, "Well, how do I dream big and fulfill those dreams?" Basically, I had to follow five steps:

Five Steps to Fulfilling Your Big Dream

- Brainstorm: First, brainstorm the possibilities. To capture potential ideas, people use little notebooks at their bedside or carry one with them. Personally, I have tried physical notebooks in the past, but I tend to lose them, or I can't find them when I need them. And when I do locate them, those potential ideas are scattered across multiple notebooks. So instead, I use what I call a "digital notebook" that is accessible on all the devices I use. My mobile phone is almost always with me, and I have a killer app called Microsoft OneNote on it.

Every time someone or something inspires me, I get a brainwave when watching a movie or reading a news article, or I feel that I might want to explore a topic any further, I make a note of it. I find that if I don't capture the idea immediately, it will more than likely fade away. If the idea shows up multiple times in my head, I put a number next to the idea. I call this list of ideas my "random sources of inspiration" list.

I organize the list by priority—moving items up and down the list, as new items get added. Every two weeks, usually on a Sunday, I open this list and sit with my coffee. If an item has occurred multiple times and I put a number next to it, I know this is something I need to pay attention to. I also pay attention to anything on the list that is repeatedly at the top.

Sometimes, I take this list and brainstorm the top ideas with a mentor or a friend I can trust, who knows me well, who knows more about the topic, or who knows someone who does. I find it critical that I know what I will prioritize and more importantly, what I will not. I limit my prioritized items that need further exploration to no more than three items at any time.

- Visualize: Next, take the item at the top of the list that you have prioritized, and visualize. Think clearly *why* you want to do it and the outcome you hope to achieve. Ask yourself if that is the outcome you really want. Is it one you are truly passionate about? One that excites you? The way I think about these questions is that I usually go for a walk to clear my mind and then visualize myself getting the task done and experiencing the thrill or satisfaction of completing that task.

You may remember my initial dream was that of running a marathon. I visualized having to train for months and put in the work, the victories I would have, and even some of the defeats—setbacks, disappointments, and injuries—that I might face. This way, I could proactively plan around how I would overcome these hurdles. (One of my favorite authors, Dan Pink, has a name for the process of thinking about everything that could go wrong and then doing all that we can to handle those issues—a "pre-mortem"—the opposite of "post-mortem.") Continuing with the visualization process, I pictured myself getting to the last mile of the marathon, grinning from ear to ear and then reaching the finish line and running into the arms of my family and friends. I visualized them telling me they were so proud of me for what I had accomplished. In my vision, I could clearly see their smiling faces, feel their hugs, and live the moment for the first time, hoping to relive it again during the marathon I planned to run someday.

My "big dream" evolved over time. Although my initial dream was to run a full marathon somewhere across America, it later became clear that I had more than one marathon in me. I "upgraded" my dream of running multiple marathons, but my idea was to run them all in the Bay Area, or across California, where I lived at the time. As I continued along that journey, though, I came across the seven-continent club and learned that a marathon was possible across every continent.

What was even more exciting was to learn that a few hundred people had done it. I "super-sized" my dream from running many marathons across America to running at least one marathon across all seven continents. I started visualizing this new super-sized dream. Can you imagine running a marathon in Antarctica among the vast landscapes of ice and water, the seals, and penguins? Or running the Big Five Marathon in Africa, which is held among the wildlife of the African savannah? The running route goes right through one of the most spectacular game reserves in Africa, and you run in the habitats of the "big five"—elephants, rhinos, buffalos, lions, and leopards. With game wardens trained to "manage" this experience, nothing separates the runners from the African wildlife. Exciting and scary at the same time, isn't it?

- Energize: Next, pick the role models, mentors, and peers who have a similar big goal and achieved the outcome or some version of it. To run a marathon, I looked up some of the greatest marathon runners of all time as well as marathon runners in my community in California. Fortunately, I came across a wonderful community of runners known as "Om Run" who not only had a large team of great mentors and coaches, but also had a group of newbies going through the same experience as me.

Surrounding myself with people in a similar mindset who had traveled a similar path that I was traversing convinced me that my goal was feasible, and I felt truly energized. Reading the stories of other long-distance runners and learning about how they achieved their big goals inspired me.

- Engage: As you validate your dreams, you may engage your mentors, family, and friends. You will need to select the right people to engage with.

> *"If you want to kill a big dream, tell it to a small-minded person."*
>
> —STEVE HARVEY

So true. I almost made that mistake a couple of times and got discouraged (albeit briefly) from pursuing my dream of running marathons across all seven continents. People who loved me dearly tried to scare me by focusing on the risks involved in running a marathon in Africa or in Antarctica. They even asked that I consider bumping up my insurance policy if I decided that I still wanted to go.

At times I almost threw in the towel, like when I read about crossing the dreaded Drake Passage, which takes about two days, and you are likely to encounter very rough seas with fifteen- to twenty-foot waves. Or when I read about the horrible sea sickness to be endured during that journey. Or about getting seriously ill on the ship or injured in Antarctica and then needing to be medically evacuated. I could go on... One of the voices in my head even told me, *I should be satisfied with running marathons across six continents. After all, it was more than most people do.* But I reminded myself that so many had successfully completed the seven-continent marathon journey, and while there was a risk that something could go awry, this was a risk I was willing to take. The unconditional support of my immediate family was a huge boost, and the encouragement from key members of my running community reminded me that anything was possible, as long as I believed in the dream.

- Execute: Now that you have figured out your big dream, visualized it, and you are energized and engaged, it is time to execute the next steps of your big dream. This is where your dream meets reality. It may not be an easy journey. It may even be painful. The most important thing to remember, though, is that every big dream is made up of many small goals. By executing consistently, you can achieve each of those small goals, and before you know it, you are on the doorstep of achieving your big dream.

Take, for example, the process of writing this book. It is a huge commitment that takes consistency, discipline, and sacrifice. When I initially thought about the writing process, having never done it before, I felt intimidated. Even overwhelmed. But then I read about it. I spoke to mentors and other authors who had written books. I clearly had to follow a process. I started by brainstorming what I wanted to write, why I wanted to write, who I was writing for, and then visualized the outcome, became energized, and finally executed by getting my "butt in the seat" to get it done. What I have learned from various authors is that the time you spend sitting down and writing—i.e., "butt in the seat"—is more valuable than just spending the time thinking about it. The execution part was the hardest, as it usually is. There are still times when I have wondered if it was easier to run marathons or to write a book about it. But just like I made that commitment to run marathons, I made a commitment to write the book, and there was no turning back.

When my friend, mentor, and role model, Dan Waldschmidt, completed the "Run Everest" challenge (also known as the "Everesting" challenge), I was truly inspired and impressed. Dan is only the tenth person on the planet to complete this incredibly difficult challenge. The idea behind the "Run Everest" is to pick a hill—any hill, anywhere in the world—and run repeats of it in a single activity until you climb over 29,000 ft (or 8,848m)—the equivalent height of Mount Everest. One activity. No time limit. No sleep. Clearly an inspiring challenge for most. But to Dan, this was his dream!

On December 10, 2018, Dan achieved his dream by running thirty-seven laps for a total of an 8,848-meter climb and over eighty-one miles run in twenty-five hours and nine minutes. What an impressive accomplishment! To this day, I am in awe of Dan and his mind-blowing achievement. Dan's dream was big. Then, he got down to chunking the big dream down to several smaller goals. In this instance, those smaller goals would be to pick increasingly harder mountains to run and successfully complete them. He continued to work on upgrading those goals and then achieving them to the point where he was then confident of fulfilling his big dream of "Run Everest." He brainstormed, visualized, got energized with his community of supporters, engaged them, and then relentlessly executed to fulfill his big dream.

Another thing worth remembering is that there is a clear rationale for breaking down your big goal into a set of smaller goals, so you are set for success. The first women's Olympic marathon champion and a pioneer in the sport, Joan Benoit Samuelson, said it best when asked why we need to break down the "pie-in-the-sky" goals into smaller goals. She states,

"By taking too big a step toward a big goal and without filling in with the short-term and intermediate goals, you are setting yourself up for failure and injury. And if you fail too many times, you are only going to be frustrated."

As I look back at my own journey, I feel that Joan was absolutely on point with this insight. After running a few marathons, I noticed a tendency for complacency that sets in. I experienced this as I got ready for my fifth marathon in Queenstown, New Zealand. As I got ready, I recall being under tremendous pressure at work as I was employed at a small startup company at the time. I ended up skimping on achieving my smaller goals (for example, consistently doing my multiple runs a week and the long runs on the weekend). I really struggled to get to the finish line during that marathon, and I risked failure and injury. I only had to learn this lesson the hard way once to not repeat it again.

Over to you now. What is your big dream? And what incremental goals can you set to achieve that dream?

"You were born with potential.
You were born with goodness and trust.
You were born with ideals and dreams.
You were born with greatness.
You were born with wings.
You are not meant for crawling, so don't.
You have wings. Learn to use them and fly."

—RUMI

Key Reflections

- What is/are your big dream(s)?

- Why do you have these big dream(s)? What led you to it?

- What has been your biggest fear or obstacle in achieving this big dream?

- What smaller, achievable, measurable goals can you set for yourself to fulfill your big dream?

- Leveraging the five-step framework, write down the relevant steps that surround your big dream and the activities and the outcomes you plan for at each step.

CHAPTER 3

REACHING HIGHER

"The greatest danger is not that we aim too high and miss it, but that we aim too low and reach it."

—MICHELANGELO

This quote has always invigorated me. And over time, I realized why!

I had seen many examples of this in my own life, starting with my childhood. A hunger to always reach higher.

When I was very young (maybe ten or eleven years old), to challenge myself, I obsessed over jumping across multiple steps at a time. I remember one instance when I tried to jump five steps at a time, each step about one foot high. These steps were built out of mosaic tiles on top of a stone foundation. They were rock solid, but how did I know that? Well, I checked the strength of that build with my forehead when I came crashing down and ended up with a huge, painful, red bump on the right side of my forehead. I cried and wailed.

I grew up in a home with four mostly rambunctious boys, and I was always curious, constantly getting into things I had no business getting into. Following that unsuccessful attempt of my own version of the Olympic long jump and high jump, I inspired my parents to try their own version of the hundred-meter sprint. Hearing my loud wails, they came running as fast as they could to my aid. I was immediately chastised by them as they consoled me, wiping away my tears. Grumpy faced and mad at myself, I mumbled a promise to not do it again. My parents reminded me that for a boy my age and my height (barely four feet at the time), jumping those steps was impossible.

Now, that was just the kind of challenge I needed.

The promise that I halfheartedly made to my parents lasted all of two weeks. It was conveniently forgotten. I was at it again. I went back to trying to jump those five steps. And this time, success.

Next, let me try six steps, I thought. And I did. The only problem was it had rained the previous night. Seconds later, I did another major faceplant, taking a bad beating on my forehead again. Darn those nasty stone steps. A shiny new red bump appeared on the other side of my forehead. All I could manage was a muffled cry. My parents always told me to count my blessings, so I did. I counted my blessings that the painful, red bump was on the opposite side of the forehead. As my parents were away from home at the time this happened, I was lucky to not get the walloping I deserved for trying this antic again. I counted my blessings a second time, this time for not having to face the wrath of my parents.

Whose idea was it to build these stone and mosaic steps anyway? I muttered to myself.

This pattern of always wanting to reach outside my comfort zone continued as I grew up. After graduating from college in India, I was among the first in my family to move farthest away from home to the other side of the planet to Michigan to pursue a master's degree in computer science. Although many thought I was crazy to move from the warm tropical climes in Bangalore, India, to the bitterly cold winters in Michigan, I was excited. Being a stranger in a strange land, I missed my family and friends very much, but the change of scenery itself didn't bother me one bit. I had arrived with two bags and two thousand dollars in loans (a huge amount by Indian standards at the time) and I was open to this experience. The move from India to North America felt like I was jumping those steps all over again.

After graduating from Michigan State University, I arrived at my first job at Bell Labs in Westminster, which was situated not far from Boulder, a blissful suburb at the foothills of Denver, Colorado (better known as the "Mile High City"). I immediately gravitated to those gorgeous mountains. They beckoned me. They teased me.

One day, someone in the community told me it was very challenging to climb the Rocky Mountains, and the hiking and climbing adventure was not for the faint of heart. These are the tallest, most intimidating mountains in Colorado with a height of over fourteen thousand feet and are fondly known as the "14ers" by the locals. To the uninitiated, climbing a 14er is fraught with many risks. The challenges could range from twisting your ankle to falling into a crevice if you don't navigate the steep twists and turns well. If you are not used to a rapid change in altitude, you risk suffering from acute mountain sickness (AMS). According to the Encyclopedia Britannica, people can suffer from the symptoms of AMS at increasing altitudes with the most serious effects felt at eight thousand feet or higher. The symptoms could include painful headaches, vomiting, tiredness, confusion, dizziness, and trouble sleeping.

One of the many benefits of living near Boulder was the accessibility to the various mountainous hikes nearby. These were smaller hills and mountains varying from six to ten thousand feet. You could leave work and hit a beautiful mountainous trail in the neighborhood in fewer than fifteen minutes. I had many favorites, but among them was the steep Mount Sanitas trails as well as the Flatiron trails.

Over fourteen months, I enjoyed hiking trails of varying lengths and altitudes. During this time, I came across an annual event sponsored by my company called the Peak Challenge. We raised funds that benefited the Emily Griffith Centers for Children. This center has done yeoman's work helping abused and troubled kids overcome debilitating challenges through education, skill building, and more.

Under the auspices of the Peak Challenge program, each sponsoring company would pick a 14er to climb that year from among the fifty-two 14ers across Colorado. Employees of a company could choose to form a team and raise funds to benefit the Emily Griffith Center. Colleagues, friends, and relatives would contribute generously, and some would even pledge a certain amount of dollars per feet climbed, motivating you to do more to help the children of the Emily Griffith Center, while taking on a personal challenge.

Through that program, I routinely started taking on increasingly difficult hikes. Some of the hikes were even arranged with the children and supervisors we were helping at the Emily Griffith Center. Getting to know the children who were directly impacted by our fundraising efforts was heartening. Through the Peak Challenge program and being inspired by the kids we impacted, I climbed over twenty-six of the 14ers across Colorado. Were the 14er climbs challenging? Of course, every one of them. Were they impossible? Of course not, not even one. "Believe, and your belief will create the fact" is an apt quote that captures this sentiment.

If all this hiking and climbing was not enough, I also got into rock and ice climbing—the real technical stuff with the ropes and all the gear. I took several months of staking out the rocks and working my way toward a respectable 5.12 climb in the rock-climbing gyms. Even to this day, I have kept my Black Diamond ice axe as a memento.

For those unfamiliar with the rating of climbs, most climbing gyms have ratings from 5.5 to 5.12. A climb rated a 5.5 is relatively easy, like climbing a ladder (a one out of ten on the difficulty scale). A 5.12 rating is like climbing a ladder with several rungs either spaced much farther apart or some rungs missing (an eight out of ten). Note that the difficulty rating can extend all the way to a 5.15, which is a more difficult climb (nine out of ten), and a six rating, which is defined as "cannot be free climbed" for most climbers. Those six-rating climbs are only for the most well-trained technical climbers.

I would have loved to try those higher rated climbs too, but none of the gyms offered them at the time. After a few months of climbing the routes within the rock gyms, I felt the pangs to get the first outdoor climb under my belt.

It was a bright, crisp sunny day, and I called my friend Tom, asking if he wanted to go out and try climbing the Half Dome in Nederland, Colorado. It was a 5.10 climb. This was going to be easier than I thought. After all, it was well below the toughest climbs I had conquered at the rock gyms. Tom had gone climbing with me at the rock gyms before, and he had always been an amazing teacher and mentor. He pushed me and others to try harder climbs when he knew we were ready. But Tom was also prudent, and he wouldn't suggest or do anything rash. I appreciated that about Tom and trusted him completely.

We got to the Half Dome. The climb looked quite doable. That's the thing. From a distance, even the toughest climb seems doable. I asked Tom what he thought. Tom vehemently agreed with me, and in his inimitable style of minimizing challenges, he said this was going to be a piece of cake. Or so we thought. Tom climbed first and had the lead rope. He was a strong climber, and it was quite hard keeping up with him. We did well for the first couple of hours and made steady progress. My hands were starting to feel tired.

When we first started climbing at the rock gyms, Tom had given me a little lesson that he had hoped I would remember for a long time to come. He said, "Satish, you see, most men, being the macho beings we are, tend to rely on our upper body strength to climb. Precisely the wrong thing to do." Pointing to one of the women who made it look easy, he continued with, "Women make such graceful and elegant climbers since they rely on their leg strength to push through." This served as a great reminder during the outdoor climb that I needed to use my own leg strength more.

Two hours later, we were nearing the summit. *This was in the bag*, I assumed. I soon realized I was wrong. Before we got to the summit, we had to navigate a lip that jutted out. We had to pull ourselves up with our arms and climb over and up onto the top. Tom made it look easy. I was next. Ten minutes passed by. My arms hesitated. My legs wavered. My heart was unconvinced. Clearly, the lesson about using your legs to climb had been forgotten, at least momentarily.

Then I looked down. That was the second lesson. "Never look backward or down when you are climbing. You will freeze," Tom had cautioned me strongly when we began the Half Dome climb earlier that morning. Well, I was more than two hundred feet up in the air, and I looked back and down beneath me.

I froze.

Today was not my day, I thought. There was no way I was going to step out and hang by the lip and then have the strength to pull myself up in the air, knowing fully well that the two-hundred-foot drop was behind me (even though there was a rope that provided some safety). Tom waited patiently. Fifteen minutes went by. I kept trying, and it got worse. My arms were giving up on me. Tom suggested that if I gave it all I got, he might be able to pull me up with the rope once I got past the lip. But I had to first do my part of pulling myself up. I tried again.

No, this is not meant to happen, I told myself. Tom was now getting anxious as the setting Colorado sun was starting to turn the sky a pink and red hue. Tom decided it was time. Now or never. He came over the top of the summit and, peering down at me, gave an ultimatum. He said, "Satish, you have a choice. You can do one of two things—climb up just like I did… or I will have to call the search and rescue team. They will charge you a nice, tidy sum of two thousand dollars to rescue you. Which option would you like?" he asked, nonchalantly.

That was all the motivation I needed. The choice between completing the climb on my own and the potential "Search and Rescue Fee" of two thousand dollars felt like *Sophie's Choice*. Although it was a matter of life and death (remember the possible two-hundred-foot fall that I had imagined?), it was less serious than the choice Sophie had to make in the movie. I quickly made up my mind, and I was up there in a jiffy.

I realized a couple of things. A lot of these obstacles are all mental. Once I got past the mind block, I was able to get through the challenge quite easily. I thanked Tom profusely that day. For staying with me. For teaching me these important lessons. For inspiring and motivating me. Years later, this mind-over-body lesson would prove to be an important one.

In 2004, my wife Deepa and I moved to Singapore as expats due to my work assignment. I missed the mountains of Denver. A lot. We lived on the thirty-fourth floor of a beautiful building in Queenstown, Singapore. *What if no real mountains or even hills existed in Singapore? There were all these tall buildings*, I reasoned. So, every Sunday, I would run up thirty-four stories. I was finding my mountain in Singapore. It took me twenty to twenty-three minutes, and it gave me the exercise and the excitement all at the same time. Not quite what I felt on the top of the 14ers in Colorado, but it was the closest thing I could find, given the concrete, high-rise jungle that I found in Singapore.

In 2012, when we arrived in California, I was introduced to running. When it came to running, although my goals were modest in the beginning, I was quickly enamored by the goal of running a marathon—thanks to the narcissistic runner who told me that running marathons was not for people like me.

It was not that I needed people to belittle me, but one of my pet peeves is being taken for granted. I had to run a marathon. Heck, I had to run more than a marathon. Why stop there? I heard about the stories of people running all seven continents. That sounded like a goal worth striving for. But many people, even those I respected, told me that my dream of running a marathon in Antarctica was challenging. Or impossible. This made it even more attractive to pursue. Of course, a small percentage of the population had already done it. They had reached higher.

You may recall Dan Waldschmidt, the tenth person on the planet to complete the Run Everest Challenge. You can't reach a higher point than Mount Everest. I had a great opportunity to speak to Dan at length a few months ago. I asked him why he reached so high and picked this incredible goal.

His response was, "Every once in a while, you need to pick a goal that scares you. Something that feels a bit out of reach.

Something that wakes that little badass within you and tells you that you still have it, and you are not an imposter. Every so often, I would question myself if I should be giving other people advice or setting the rules. And when I do things like Run Everest, it bolsters the idea that I still have it."

In the introduction of this book, I had reminisced about how I imagined that my marathon goal was impossible. Reaching Higher was among the first steps that got me going on that journey to "I'm possible."

Now, it is your turn.

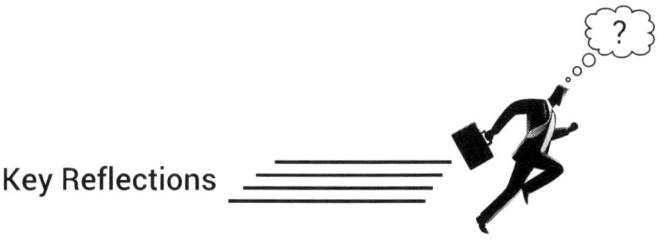

Key Reflections

- Write down one (or more) goal(s) that scare you.

- Write down three things you will be willing to attempt as a goal (these could include things you have never attempted before or attempted and failed).

- What is something that makes you feel like an imposter? Why does it make you feel like an imposter? Is there anything you could do to overcome that feeling?

CHAPTER 4

SHOWING UP

"When you show up and keep putting your work out there, good things start to happen. You make new connections, people reach out to you, opportunities start to present themselves."

—AYODE JI AWOSKA

They say the third time is the charm. I had hit the snooze button a third time, but the charm didn't work. Somehow, getting out of bed that morning seemed more challenging than most Saturday mornings reserved for my long runs while training for a marathon.

According to the author Eric Weiner, even the great stoic Marcus Aurelius, who ruled the Roman Empire from 120 to 180 AD, was not spared the "getting out of bed" challenge. Marcus had thought more deeply about this "problem," even taking it to the point of exploring the various motivations of getting out of bed as any great philosopher would. Eric Weiner, who wrote the book *The Socrates Express,* summarizes this quandary. Marcus saw the act of getting out of bed as a choice between "duty" and "obligation." "Duty comes from the inside; obligation comes from the outside," Marcus had concluded. When we act with a sense of duty (i.e., our *why*), we voluntarily lift ourselves and others around us. When we act out of obligation, we tend to shield ourselves. Only ourselves. That morning, my own conclusion was that my getting out of bed was part *duty* and part *obligation.* Marcus would have been proud.

> *"People are anxious to improve their circumstances but unwilling to improve themselves; they therefore remain bound."*
>
> —JAMES ALLEN

Just two more minutes, I told myself, wanting to go back to sleep so badly. It felt like I was trying to prove James Allen right. And then, it hit me like a ton of bricks; my running group met at 6 a.m. sharp, and the clock was already careening toward 5:15 a.m. *Early is on time, and on time is late,* our running group leader's cautionary words echoed in my head. Now, I was fully awake. I leaped out of bed and made a mad dash to the bathroom at a pace that would have made Usain Bolt proud.

All the ruckus I had created startled my wife, Deepa. I heard her muttering, half-awake, "Is this the big one?" she asked.

"Not yet, honey," I shouted back. We lived in Northern California, and of course Deepa was referring to the Damocles

Sword (Cicero, 46 BC) of the next big earthquake that always hung above us.

Fortunately, I had made it a habit to at least pull out my running clothes the prior night and place them on the dresser in the bedroom. While every long run required an extensive warm-up and stretching, the sprint to the kitchen was all the warm-up I could get prior to my run that morning. Glancing at my watch, I was momentarily proud. Nine minutes and fifty-four seconds is all it took to brush and get ready. But then, I reminded myself that waking up a little earlier would have been the better option to avoid all the palpitations in my chest because of my just-in-time approach.

In the kitchen, all I had time for that morning was a banana and a protein bar, washed down with "dip-dip" chai. In case you are wondering what a "dip-dip chai" is, it's the style of chai tea bags that you can dip repeatedly into hot water and optionally add milk and sugar at the end to give you what seems like tea-flavored hot water; no offense to tea drinkers who like to drink tea this way. Growing up in India, making chai meant an extensive ritual, using select, hand-picked tea leaves with an extensive brewing process, finished with milk and sugar.

After getting a helping of the sustenance, I was out of the house in a flash. It was now 5:40 a.m. I had a twelve- to fifteen-minute drive to the running trail. *Phew. Maybe I will still make it to the trail in time*, I reassured myself. I also promised to do better next Saturday—the same promise that I have made for five Saturdays in a row. On my drive, a brain wave struck. *Maybe, I should set the clock five to ten minutes forward*. But that brain wave would have to wait.

I had arrived at the start of the running trail at Campbell Park at 5:52 a.m.

The first lesson or insight I had was the importance of showing up.

As Melanie Pinola shares in her article, the great American painter Chuck Close said it best:

> *"Inspiration is for amateurs—the rest of us just show up and get to work."*
>
> —CHUCK CLOSE

Showing up can mean different things to different people.

- For several folks, it is the very act of arriving at a place.

- For others, it is not only to arrive, but also to be fully present.

- For an even smaller subset, it is to arrive, be fully present, and be fully prepared to put in the work, regardless of what obstacles exist, including the naysaying mind.

- Finally, there are an eclectic few who show up not only for themselves in the way that I described above, but also for others.

This final nuance of what it meant to "show up" dawned on me when I was speaking to one of my mentor runners Ranga, who had also been mentoring other runners for more than a decade. I was curious to know why he kept mentoring and why he was showing up the way he did every single weekend? *What did he get for showing up early every Saturday morning for these runs?* I wondered.

"Doesn't this showing up for mentoring people again and again get old?" I asked him. Before he had a chance to respond, I followed with, "Didn't sharing the same concepts with new runners over time get exhausting?"

He thought for a moment, paused, and simply responded that he could see that his showing up was clearly making an impact to others. "That drives me," he said, his eyes growing moist with emotion. He added, "In that process though, I have gained a lot more than I have given." He shared the sense of fulfillment he felt when he saw the impact he had made over the years, which kept him wanting to do even more. The continued learning and growing in the process also helped.

Wow—what an amazing concept! I thought to myself.

Showing up can be challenging. Maybe you had a late night of partying, or if you're a runner, you didn't put in the needed running mileage during the week because you let your naysaying mind reinforce your self-limiting beliefs. Or it was raining. Or it was sunny. Or you were feeling exhausted. Or lazy. Or because you had to water your plants. Or something absurd. There is always an excuse. Some are creative. And some are even believable.

Magic happens when you show up no matter—whether you are unsure, scared, unprepared, exhausted, defeated, or don't feel like it. When it comes to running marathons or a project at work or at home, you create sustained success by building on incremental victories. These victories come from... you guessed it, showing up! Also, when I first started running marathons, I started thinking about what was in my control and what was outside my control. I couldn't control the weather, running gear failing unexpectedly, potential for accidents on the trail, etc. Showing up, on the other hand, was clearly within my control.

I have carried this lesson about showing up, being prepared, putting in the work, and giving it my 100 percent not just on the running trails, but also to my workplace and to my home. As a business professional, showing up prepared has helped me feel fully engaged in the work that I am doing, get ample rewards and recognition, and drive better outcomes for myself, my colleagues, and the business. Showing up at home has meant that I can be a loving parent, a devoted husband, a better brother, a responsible son.

Showing up means being dependable, consistent, and committed to the cause. I once heard this gem of a saying:

> *"You can't be a writer if you don't write. You can't be a chef if you never cook. You can't be an athlete if you never train."*

It all starts by showing up.

Key Reflections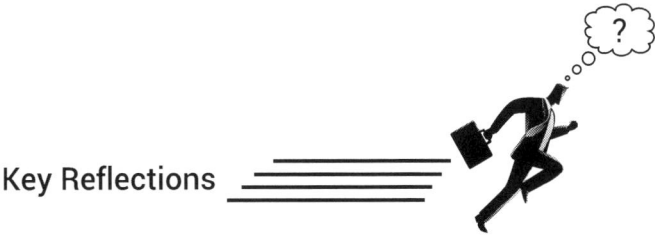

- What does it mean for you to "show up"?

- Pick an activity and write down specifically how you will prepare to show up.

- If it is an activity that requires *consistently* showing up, how are you going to hold yourself accountable to keep showing up the way you want to every time?

PART 2

THE PRINCIPLES

CHAPTER 5

MINDSET

MAKING A MOLEHILL OUT OF A MOUNTAIN
June 20, 2002, Thiruvarppu Temple (South India).

My wife Deepa and I were gallivanting around Kerala, India, on our honeymoon and visiting a beautiful, historic temple with over 1,500 years of heritage, history, rituals, and practices that have stood the test of time. Right inside that temple, we came across the mightiest of beasts in the animal kingdom.

"Won't it cut the rope and run rampant, just like we see in the movies?" I asked Babu, the *mahout* (elephant keeper) in amazement.

Beaming with a toothless smile, Babu quipped, "Well, he won't because he *thinks* he cannot." Babu waved his index finger up in the air next to my face, to emphasize a strong *no*. Just then, Manikandan, the elephant ("Mani" for short, as Babu fondly called him), seemed to nod in agreement about eight feet away.

When Deepa and I came across this majestic beast at this magnificent temple, Mani was bound to a thick, metal pole with a somewhat simple, flimsy rope. Babu went on, "When Mani was a baby, we tied one of his legs with a rope like this one. He tried to escape many a time, but the rope held him back. As he got older, he stopped trying," Babu laughed loudly, as the red juice of betel leaves he was chewing on plotted its own escape from one corner of his open mouth.

Mani was a special elephant, a caparisoned temple elephant. You could tell this because he had a thick red velvet cloth (known as the "caparison") with garish golden decorations coming down his forehead, stopping midway through his trunk. This flamboyant piece of elephant jewelry was held in place by a thick rope going around his neck, hidden out of view by its large flapping ears. A row of cheerful bells would jingle at the top of the caparison every time Mani moved. This story of the "elephant and the rope" sounded so familiar. After thinking about it a bit more, I realized my uncle had regaled me with a similar story when I visited the circus as a child many moons ago. Now, here it was, in front of my eyes in full splendor—a humongous, mellow beast trapped by a belief that a flimsy rope could curb its freedom.

April 2014, San Diego, California.

A new time. A new place. A new animal. A new lesson.

"Yes!" came the loud, quick reply along with squeals of excitement. I had asked my children, Snigdha and Sandeep, a couple times if they were sure they wanted to sit in the "splash zone" at Sea World, San Diego.

Now, I asked them a final time, "Are you sure?"

"Yes, Dad!" they answered, almost admonishing me for asking them again. They were exhilarated at the thought of getting soaked by the killer whales (or orcas) as we waited for the show to start.

About halfway through the show, with a shiver running down my spine from being completely drenched, it became abundantly clear to me that the orcas were obediently executing every move commandeered by their handlers. This was an eye-opening experience that demonstrated to me what was possible at the other end of the spectrum from the self-limiting beliefs I had witnessed in Mani, the elephant.

Later, after the show, I spoke to one of the handlers, Jane. I was wondering how they were able to make these six-thousand-pound giants do all those "tricks" at their beck and call. Jane immediately corrected me, gently reminding me that these were not "tricks." Rather, they were "learned behaviors." She emphasized how the orcas are painstakingly trained over several months with loads of patience using incremental steps, positive reinforcement, and rewards. She also shared that there were multiple types of trainers, including those who do research on the orcas, work on interactions, and focus on their care, who make all of this possible.

When I recalled both of these experiences, the one with the elephant and the other with the orcas, I remember being keen to know what drove the orca and elephant to behave the way they did. What I didn't know then was how these experiences would impact me decades later. As I pondered this further, two things bubbled up to the surface: the power of *belief* and its close cousin, *mindset,* and how they ultimately become your destiny!

A well-known quote often attributed to the Mahatma sums this up nicely.

> *"Your beliefs become your thoughts.*
> *Your thoughts become your words.*
> *Your words become your actions.*
> *Your actions become your habits.*
> *Your habits become your values.*
> *Your values become your destiny."*

—MAHATMA GANDHI

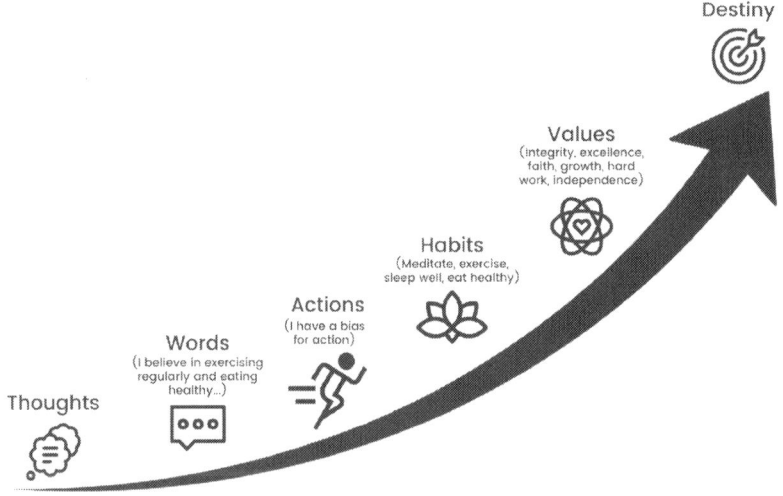

From Beliefs to Destiny

What is "mindset," you ask?

Mindset is a belief about certain traits in humans, often referred to as their TICs—talents, intelligence, or capabilities, as the well-known Stanford psychologist, Dr. Carol Dweck, has referred to in her research on mindset (Dweck, 2008). Mindset is what determines how you take on challenges, how you push your limits, or how you overcome obstacles.

According to Dr. Dweck, two kinds of mindset exist: fixed and growth. People with a fixed mindset believe TICs are inherent traits; either you have something or you don't. Those with a growth mindset believe your TICs can develop or grow, like a muscle!

We are all guilty of having a fixed mindset at times. For many years, I used to think I didn't have musical talent. My wife and children would wholeheartedly agree with that notion, especially as it relates to my vocal talent, given my atrocious bathroom singing. But then, I decided to give playing the piano a shot, and my children Snigdha and Sandeep encouraged me. I was pleasantly surprised to hear my daughter (who is a straight shooter) tell me that I had the ability to learn the piano quickly.

Maybe you think you don't have a mind for numbers, you think you simply don't have the stamina to be a runner, or it is too scary or risky to take your idea and create your own startup. The truth is there are few things you cannot accomplish through continuous learning and determined practice. Essentially, you can develop and grow your TICs—your talent, intelligence, and capabilities. I am convinced that even my bathroom singing could improve through a motivated voice coach.

The question is, do you have a fixed mindset or a growth mindset?

Let's examine the differences between the two:

Fixed Mindset	Growth Mindset
Belief that talent, intelligence and capabilities are traits you are born with	Belief that talent, intelligence and capabilities are traits you can change with effort
Focused on the outcome	Focused on the process
Gives up easily based on belief that you either have it or you don't	Don't give up easily as anything can be learned
Feels threatened by others' success	Feels inspired by others' success
Make excuses since they can never be good at something through effort	Celebrate even small successes since they know it is the foundation of larger wins
Avoids new challenges for fear of failure and gives up easily when setbacks are encountered	Welcomes new challenges and persist despite setbacks

Fixed versus Growth Mindset

Having the right mindset is critical to take on challenging goals. Award-winning TEDx speaker Preston Pugmire had perhaps the best description of the three stages of developing the right mindset:

- Stage one: It is possible, but for someone else.

- Stage two: It is possible for me, but how?

- Stage three: It is inevitable for me; now let's get it done.

The Three Stages of Mindset Development

When I initially thought of running a marathon, I felt it was something that someone else could do, but not me—this is the "it is possible, but for someone else" stage of your mindset. This is where the story of Mani and the orcas made a comeback. It occurred to me that there was a simple, proverbial rope holding me back from what was possible.

Then, I started seeing similar people around me who were giving running a shot and making progress. With some work, these people were hitting milestones like a half marathon or a marathon. This increased my confidence, and the proverbial rope holding me back began to unravel. This got me to the second stage of mindset change, the "it is possible for me, but how?" stage.

My introduction to the Om Run group and meeting the amazing mentors I bonded with made all the difference to the continued evolution in my mindset. I started by attempting a short run, and it felt good. Slowly but surely, over several weeks and months, with the support of mentors, coaches, and peers, I increased my running distance to five kilometers (3.1 miles), then gradually worked toward ten kilometers (6.2 miles). I did a couple of 5K and 10K races with my peer group that bolstered my confidence even more.

Then, I attempted getting to the half marathon distance of twenty-one kilometers (13.1 miles). That was not easy. It took a few months of determined practice before we could get there. A few of us decided to run the Oakland Half Marathon in March 2012. It was an uplifting experience, especially doing that as a group. While we had "conquered" a half marathon, coming out of the Oakland half marathon, some of us decided we could possibly do a full marathon. We were still at the "it is possible for me, but how?" stage of the mindset change, but this time with respect to a full marathon. However, completing the Oakland half marathon had given me the buoyancy and the confidence I needed to move further toward my goal of running a full marathon.

Following that, we continued more running and training. It took me a few more months. While at times I had some doubts about my own abilities, through blood, sweat, and some tears, I almost made it all the way to running the marathon distance of about forty kilometers (or twenty-four miles) during practice runs. I had successfully arrived at the final stage of "it is inevitable for me; now, let's get it done" stage. Signing up for the San Francisco marathon (one of the toughest in the US with its undulating course) and then successfully completing it was the milestone I needed to keep going! Some people have asked me why I signed up for this marathon knowing fully well that it was among the toughest across the US. I did this for several reasons: This marathon was the next one coming up, and many in the Om Run group I was training with had signed up; I thought it would be fun to train and achieve this milestone as a group, with some of the mentors and peers I had known. A part of me also wanted to challenge myself, especially after some people actively discouraged me from signing up for this race.

After having successfully run the San Francisco marathon, a story that caught my attention and imagination was that of Chau Smith, a marathoner. Chau had not only run marathons across all seven continents (and become part of the "Seven-Continent Club") but had also run those seven continents in seven days, becoming a part of the "Triple Seven Quest" (Hung, 2017). If all this was not enough, Chau did all this at seventy-five years old—a truly incredible inspiration!

Chau moved from Vietnam after her family faced incredibly difficult challenges with the French executing her father in 1947, forcing her mother into hiding, who then gave birth to Chau there. Chau's mother was only able to record her birth when she felt it was safe, which was about three years after her birth. Chau got exposed to running in her forties, first by biking behind her husband Michael, who was a marathon runner. And then when she started her own business, she started having severe back and neck pain due to the financial and emotional stress. To get some relief from the stress, she started running with her husband. Like most runners I know, Chau loved traveling too. She and her husband started combining the two hobbies, and before she knew it, she was able to complete marathons across all seven continents. Most people would be satisfied at this point. But not Chau. When she heard about the Triple Seven Quest, she readily signed up for it and got it done in her seventies. She continues to run to this day.

With my love of travel and having experienced the runners' high after completing the tough San Francisco marathon, the Seven-Continent Club seemed like an enticing challenge. Cutting the proverbial rope that had held me back seemed within reach. Preston Pugmire's "three-stage mindset" tool, which made running my first marathon inevitable, now made my seven-continent marathon goal inevitable as well. However, the stakes this time were much higher. The journey was much longer. The planning and execution needed were much greater. Even so, this journey had become inevitable.

The magic of mindset feels like an amazing discovery, almost like a cure for cancer (which I wish there was). With the right mindset, anything is possible—even running marathons across every continent for an overweight, forty-two-year-old who had hardly run before. Not even a beer run.

So, what is your mindset? Which stage are you in? Imagine the possibilities and where will it take you next!

Key Reflections

- Would you say you have a fixed or growth mindset? Think about specific examples and why you think so!

- What is an activity or goal that you have felt was outside your realm of achievement? Apply the three-stage mindset tool and explore where you are in that journey.

- If you are stuck on either step one or two of the three-stage mindset transformation, what can you do to get to the next stage?

CHAPTER 6

IT TAKES A VILLAGE

"Go fast. Go alone. Go far. Go together."

—AFRICAN PROVERB

This feels like a quote made for long distance running, an initiative at work, or a community project in your city or county.

They say it takes a village to create the most amazing individuals and deliver the most inspiring outcomes. Like most people I know, I always thought of running as an individual sport. My belief was that while some coaching was needed to help the athlete, running relied on the individual's ability to succeed. I no longer believe that. I have realized that it takes an entire village of mentors, peers, and family members to make those amazing achievements possible, whether it is in running or another individual "sport," like writing a book or making a startup company successful.

Let's now further examine those various stakeholders within a "village" and talk about creating your own village if one doesn't exist for you just yet. If your village does exist, congratulations! Stick around and review this chapter, as what I share may help make your village better.

| Mentors | Coaches | Peers | Family & Friends |

Who Is in Your Village?

MENTORS

Mentors have had a truly outsized, positive impact on my professional and personal life.

The impact of mentors on my long-distance running cannot be overstated. I fondly call them my "tribe." They are sometimes referred to as coaches, but we will discuss the difference between mentors and coaches later in this chapter.

When I think of mentors, I think of both *active* and *passive* mentors. Active mentors are directly and personally engaged with you and fully vested in your success and outcomes, while passive mentors are usually not directly engaged (and, in some cases, may not even be alive), yet they inspire you and can still have an outsized impact on your life and outcomes.

ACTIVE MENTORS

Active mentors are typically with you throughout your journey until you get across that finish line, and most often, even beyond. They are the subject matter experts. They are caring, respectful, experienced, knowledgeable, committed, and dependable. Active mentors can also take on different roles based on where you are in your journey, and you can have more than one active mentor at the same time. They may be cheerleaders, who cheer you on no matter what; sponsors, who pull you or push you up to achieve a goal; or critics, who provide the constructive feedback you need to course correct and make meaningful progress. In the end, active mentors are all about "caring and sharing" and helping you accelerate your learning, but each mentor type does it in their own way.

Thanks to the active mentors in my running journey, I learned very quickly how to pace myself, how to eat right as a runner, how to avoid injuries, and if I did injure myself, how to take care of myself to minimize the downtime while staying healthy for the long term.

Cheerleaders   Sponsors   Critics

Types of Active Mentors

You may recall that I previously spoke about one of my mentors, Ranga, who always said, "Early is on time; on time is late!" We used to joke around that he and other mentors were less mentors, and more "tormentors." As much as I initially felt guilty if I did not arrive early for a run, it took some time for the fact to sink in that he was right about the need for us to be punctual and, ideally, a bit early. When a runner in the group is tardy, they upend the flow and create disruption and consternation. They are always trying to catch up, but most of them never do. They don't get a full pre-run stretch as they should. And since they don't stretch pre-run, they don't get warmed up. If they don't get warmed up, then most of them find it challenging to keep up with the rest of the group. They struggle a lot. With the running group ethos of "no runner left behind," this has a domino effect on the group and could easily ruin the rhythm and flow for the group. There is a great parallel here when you think of tardiness associated with showing up for meetings and its impact on people within the meeting and for those joining late.

Besides instilling in us the importance of punctuality, I would like to share another specific running lesson that has stayed with me for almost a decade. This lesson has had a significant, long-term impact on my running abilities. But the reason I share this is the value of mentors in accelerated learning and how it possibly changed the course of my running.

It was the day of my first run that I described in a previous chapter. We had planned to run for two miles. As we neared the one-mile mark, we needed to navigate a challenging hill on the trail with 12 percent or more grade. Being new to running, I was doing my best to keep pushing myself up the hill, but I was running out of breath, just trying to keep up. One of my mentors, Prasana, saw my struggle, ran alongside, and pulled up right beside me.

"Pump your arms, and your legs will follow," he said.

"What?" I responded, between gasps of breathlessness.

"Pump your arms," he said as he showed me how by moving his arms back and forth.

A bit of explanation might be in order here. When we walk or run, we swing our arms. As you take that next step, you tend to swing the opposite arm. This helps us keep our bodies balanced and enables us to move in a straight line. Because your arms and legs counter each other, pumping your arms faster will cause you to speed up.

I later learned that this running technique is commonly used by sprinters rather than long distance runners. For long distance runners, though, this technique could be a savior when it comes to navigating uphill, since it helps you power up that hill. Having taken some flying classes a couple decades ago when I had some aspirations to become a pilot, I wish to share an example that truly depicts the kind of impact this "pumping of the arms" had on me.

Imagine you are flying the plane and going down as if to land, and the instructor decides to turn the engine off. If you try to go into the air again at this point, the plane will struggle until you turn the engine back on again. Then, a sudden rush of energy propels you into the sky. To this day, when I am tackling an uphill on my run, I think of this technique.

Now, take this and relate it to something you do at work that you have found difficult. What can a mentor teach you that can help you deal with your own "uphill"? For example, maybe you have a problem with making meetings productive. A mentor might tell you that you need to publish an agenda ahead of time, identify a role for every attendee (no "spectators"), and identify and get aligned around the outcome(s) you want to achieve together for that meeting. Would that make your meetings more productive? You bet!

PASSIVE MENTORS

This type of mentor does not even have to be alive to qualify. These are the individuals who have inspired you and whose life-changing insights you have gained from—whether that's guidance on how to complete a task, inspiration on why you should keep going, or someone you simply want to follow in their footsteps. They may not know us, but we know them. We admire them. Some of us may even worship them. Think about Steve Jobs, motivational speaker Jim Rohn, the boxer Muhammad Ali. You may have read about them or learned about them through word of mouth. You may have watched their YouTube videos, heard their podcasts, or read their books. They have inspired millions among us.

For the longest time, many people tried to break the barrier of running the four-minute mile but failed. And then Roger Bannister tried and succeeded. To this day, thinking of Roger Bannister's achievement gives me goosebumps (AMA,

October 2000). Although his record only lasted forty-six days, he was the first person to show that the seemingly impossible goal was actually possible. He lived in a different time and place, but it is fair to say that he inspires hordes of runners across the globe to this day.

When it comes to marathons and running them across the seven continents, one of my favorite passive mentors is Chau Smith, whom I mentioned in the previous chapter. To serve as a reminder, Chau ran seven marathons across seven continents in seven days, and she is seventy-five years old. Chau's "never-say-die" attitude fascinated me, starting with the bomb blast she survived when she was thirteen; she had shrapnel in her arm and leg all her life. She says the shrapnel causes pain, even today, but she has never let anyone or anything dictate where she is going with her life, and nothing seems to stop her!

COACHES

Coaches are a common fixture in the world of sports. A football or soccer coach may have never played a game in their life, yet they are amazing coaches. A coach does not have to be the subject matter expert. While some basic knowledge of the subject (in this case, the rules of football or soccer) is needed, they mostly need to understand what makes people tick and how to get the best out of them.

Coaches seem to be omnipresent these days. They cover a wide variety of subjects, from voice coaching to coaching you on your business, communication, confidence, and happiness. I have come across various types of coaches in my life, and it blew my mind when I learned there are coaches for almost every discipline you can think of. I count myself among the most open-minded folks, but an "intimacy coach"? That feels a bit awkward to me.

For your reference on the coaching possibilities, here is the list of thirty-one types of coaches from the coaching-online.org website.

1. behavioral coach
2. business coach
3. career coach
4. career-transition coach
5. confidence coach
6. empowerment coach
7. executive coach
8. group coach
9. happiness coach
10. high-performance coach
11. inspirational coach
12. intimacy coach
13. wellness coach
14. intuitive coach
15. leadership coach
16. life coach
17. life-transition coach
18. mental-health coach
19. organizational coach
20. performance coach
21. personal development coach
22. personality coach
23. relationship coach

24. self-love coach
25. skills coach
26. social coach
27. somatic coach
28. strategy coach
29. success coach
30. team coach
31. transformation coach

I like this list because when I first saw it, it exposed me to the various possibilities to achieve specific outcomes through the power of coaching. I am sharing this list in the hope that it helps you too.

I have personally benefited greatly from having a running coach who doubled as a mentor. I have also benefited professionally from an executive coach I hired and from an organizational coach my company brought in to help us and our teams achieve our objectives. The thing that struck me about my coaches is the questions they asked. They set clear expectations with milestones. They made me think. They prodded me when I went off course. They knew how to appeal to my higher senses. They knew what made me tick. In the end, they helped me achieve my goals and more. A good coach or mentor is worth their weight in gold.

MENTORS VERSUS COACHES

Mentors and coaches serve their own purpose at different stages of your learning and development journey, whether in running, in your career, or in life. To accelerate learning and development over the long term and to help you develop your whole self, a mentor can be an invaluable asset. However, if you have a short-term, specific need or goal, then a coach is an incredible resource. In the end, it all depends on what you want to accomplish and how quickly you want to get there.

While you can clearly leverage a mentor, a coach, or both, this table below helps further clarify each of their roles and helps you leverage them appropriately.

Mentor	Coach
Provide advice based on experience - The mentee is the one that drives any action	Co-create actionable plans to achive the objectives
A less formally structured or compensated resource	Typically a fully structured, paid-for resource
Focuses on the overall development of the individual	Focuses on achieving specific objectives
Subject Matter Expert	Not necessarily an Subject Matter Expert
Usually for the long term	Typically time bound or short term
Agenda, Timline, etc driven by the mentee	Drives the agenda, timeline, etc.
Agenda is open	Agenda is typically set
Go to for answers	Gets the answers out of you

Mentor versus Coach

PEERS

> *"You are the average of the five people you spend the most time with."*
>
> —JIM ROHN, MOTIVATIONAL SPEAKER

My interpretation of Jim's eloquent quote was that part of our progress is greatly impacted by people we surround ourselves with. This is especially true for those of us who are largely triggered by extrinsic motivation.

Peers are the most accessible, approachable, and ubiquitous source of motivation. We all know the most effective peer support groups are those that provide knowledge, share experiences, and beget emotional, social, or practical support to each other. A peer is able to offer support by virtue of their relevant experience; they have "been there, done that" and can relate to others who are now in a similar situation. While the mentor is typically seen as a role model and is sometimes put on a pedestal due to their achievements or their stature in a group, with a peer, you are creating a shared experience. Surrounding yourself with the right kind of peers can be an uplifting, rewarding experience.

The power of peers became apparent to me early in my running journey. Let me illustrate this power with a story. Our weekend-long runs used to be early on Saturday morning, sometimes starting as early as 5 or 5:30 a.m. Most of the time, we would run in a large group of twenty to twenty-five people. But if there were time constraints, then we would choose to break off from the group and run in a smaller group of three to four people. As hard as I tried to get to bed early on a Friday night, I would sometimes have a late night. When the alarm rudely woke me up at 4:15 or 4:30 a.m., I would be tempted to hit the snooze button. But then I would remember that my peers (and if running with a larger group, both my mentors and peers) would be waiting for me.

The funny thing is that when I expressed this to my running peers, we quickly realized we "showed up" because of that sense of commitment we felt for each other. I showed up for my peers, and they showed up for me. That is one clear demonstration of the power of peers.

When you are trying to pick up a new skill, the learning curve is steep. Running was no different. While mentors were on hand to help us in our growth, it was our peers we tested our assumptions with or asked questions that we were not comfortable asking our mentors. My peers also shared their lessons learned and the new things they tried—maybe it was a new kind of shoe, a new electrolyte supplement, a new cap or water bottle, all of which accelerated our learning and adaptation as a group and drove our success.

Running as a group played a big role in my accomplishments. If our pace was similar, we would run together. But, when someone was not having a particularly good day or they had an injury or were just feeling down, it was our peers who would help pull each other up. There also a sense of friendly competition between peers who help each other show what was possible and change our mindset. We also celebrated each other's success as a group, and that created an incredible bond between us and made the success more special.

FAMILY

The marathon is a journey full of ups and downs, literally and figuratively. The family is the foundation, the "lynchpin" of your journey as it was in my case.

Training for a marathon takes away so much time from your family. Think of all the hours of running you spend just on your weekly runs. I remember spending an average of forty to fifty hours a week at the peak of my training. If I included the time it took to travel back and forth to my running trail, bump that up to an average of fifty to sixty hours away from my family every single week. Sacrifices are made by your spouse, children, parents, siblings, and others who may not see you at breakfast for months or miss you at family gatherings. You may have to be absent from a child's soccer practice, their dance event, or a weekend swim meet while your spouse or partner picks up the slack. All of these add up over time since training for a marathon could last at least four to six months.

When it comes to running marathons across seven continents, you take this level of commitment and unconditional support that you need from the family several notches higher. There is the travel, dealing with the logistics in your absence, and the anxiety that they feel for you as you navigate all things foreign to you. Unless the family is traveling with you (in my case, they traveled with me to three of the seven continents), my spouse and children were left behind for at least several days or sometimes even several weeks (like when I went to Antarctica). My wife had to manage the family, do the grocery or other shopping for essentials, take care of the kids, take care of the home, and keep wondering how I was doing in a land far away from America.

I always knew running a marathon in Antarctica was going to be incredibly demanding. But the bigger challenge was getting there. Over two days, you have to cross one of the roughest bodies of water called the Drake Passage. The Drake's fifteen- to twenty-foot-high waves have swallowed many ships in its icy cold depths. I was concerned about the risks, and I approached my wife, who said, "I married you because you had bold dreams. Go for it."

While my wife put on a brave face as I left on my adventure, she continued to be anxious about my safety. She told me after I returned that she had found out the very ship I was on for the two weeks of my Antarctica sojourn had taken on water in the Arctic the previous summer. Nobody could contact me when I was on my journey, especially during the fourteen days on the ship. So, I cannot even imagine the kind of anxiety she went through during that time. I feel so fortunate to have that kind of unconditional support from my wife and family. She and my children are a big part of my success.

MY VILLAGE

Running marathons across the world is a life-altering experience. Although on the surface it feels like a fiercely individual sport, nothing could be further from the truth in terms of the contributions my "village" had to my success.

I once heard this wonderful saying:

> *"If you want something, dream, dare, and do. But if you want something extraordinary, dream, dare, and do with your community."*

My amazing village of family and friends, peers, coaches, and mentors helped me do extraordinary things. I simply cannot imagine that it would've been possible without them.

CREATING YOUR OWN VILLAGE

Now that you have heard a fair bit about my village, time to check in and learn about your village. If you want to create a village of mentors, coaches, peers, family, and friends for running, work, or pursuing any of your passions, stick around for the remaining part of this chapter to learn more. If you already have a vibrant village, I can assure you can still benefit from what I share here:

- First, understand your "why": Why are you doing what you are doing? If this is regarding running, do you want to run because you want to improve your physical fitness, to lose weight, to have mental peace, or to honor another person? If this is a project tied to your profession, then why are you doing this project or activity? To increase your income? To learn a new skill? For a promotion?

- Define SMART goals: SMART goals are specific, measurable, achievable, relevant and time bound. For example, if I say I want to lose twenty-five pounds, that is not a SMART goal. But if I said, I would like to lose twenty-five pounds by Christmas Day this year, I can measure and record progress every week using my scale. I will aim to lose about two pounds a week, and since I am five feet, eight inches and 180 pounds, losing twenty-five pounds feels like a good goal (and much needed).

- A mentor, a coach, or both: If you are working on a long-term personal development goal, then a mentor may be more appropriate. If you have a specific, time-bound, performance goal, then a coach might be more appropriate. Refer to the table describing a mentor versus coach if you need help with this topic.

- Finding a mentor or coach: Many are baffled by how to find a mentor or coach. Look for experts related to the skill or industry. Speak to your work colleagues, friends, family members. Look on LinkedIn, Twitter, Instagram. Go to a meetup in your area or online. Join an industry group or a running group in your area.

- Be curious: Prepare to engage with those experts. Know your why. Be clear about your goals (long term and short term). Ask thoughtful questions. Follow up. Ask those experts for three or five people they recommend you speak to.

- Give before you take: If you are engaging a mentor, try to understand them, their background, and how you could possibly help them before you ask for their help. Is there a project you can help them on? Is there a charity or cause they care about? Could you contribute your skills or service there? Could you volunteer for a project they want to get launched?

- Be grateful: Thank anyone who helps you promptly. Be genuinely grateful about the help you receive and their willingness to help. Send thank you notes or call them.

Even better, reciprocate in ways that help the person who helped you.

- Keep showing up: Keep showing up week after week. Learn names. Build friendships. Share your passion and learn theirs. Be fully committed. Show up on time. Give it all you got.

- Be open to possibilities: Things are not always guaranteed to go according to plan. If you are unable to keep up or have your eye on something else (for example, you are training for a marathon but feel that at this stage, a half marathon or a triathlon may be more appropriate for you), be clear with your mentor, coach, or peer.

- Stay in touch: If someone helped you along your journey, stay in touch. Even if they are not part of your journey anymore. If they reach out for help, be willing to help. They say what goes around comes around. It sure will. It is just a matter of time.

I feel fortunate to have a village I can call my own. We form unbreakable bonds through shared experiences. This community is uplifting and inspiring. It keeps me going. It has made extraordinary things possible for me.

My wish for you is the same.

Key Reflections

- Have you had a mentor or a coach in your life? What impact have they had?

- Was the mentor a cheerleader, a sponsor, or a critic? Have you had multiple mentors at one time?

- Write down three active mentors and three passive mentors in your life. Share the areas of your life they impacted.

- Have you created your own village or community? Are you part of someone else's village?

- Do you have all three important elements in your village or someone else's village that you are part of—mentors, coaches, and peers?

CHAPTER 7

PREPARATION

"Give me six hours to chop down a tree, and I will spend the first four hours sharpening the axe."

—ABRAHAM LINCOLN

Such a great quote on the importance of preparation. I have tried to incorporate this sentiment highlighting the need for diligent preparation into the various aspects of my life. In running. At home. At work.

Preparing for a marathon feels like getting ready for any major medium-or-long-term project. Take, for example, planning for a critical product launch at a large enterprise; or planning to launch a startup; or practicing for a crucial concert as an artist. You get the idea. Preparation involves planning and designing with a goal in mind, a time-bound program with milestones, and consistent execution to deliver on outcomes measured by key performance indicators (KPIs).

In the first part of this chapter, we will cover the preparation involved for a marathon, and in the second half, we will draw parallels to prepare for the other "marathons" in our lives, such as launching a startup. We will also examine the top-ten obstacles in effective preparation and how to overcome them.

Preparation for a marathon lasts sixteen to eighteen weeks and incorporates several foundational elements. These elements include combining five types of runs repeated over multiple days in a week to build your endurance—race pace runs, speed runs, tempo runs, long runs, and recovery runs. Strength training and cross training are additional elements that boost running capacity and help improve overall conditioning and athletic performance.

Race pace means you run for twenty to thirty seconds at or below the pace at which you intend to run your race. So, if you want to run your marathon at an average of ten minutes a mile then your pace for this run would be between ten minutes and ten and a half minutes per mile.

Tempo runs are at twenty to thirty seconds faster than race pace. Continuing the prior example, you would run your tempo run at a pace between nine and a half minutes and ten minutes.

Sprints or speed runs are done at a much higher pace and typically can go two to three minutes higher than your intended race pace but kept to shorter distances. With an intended ten-minute-per-mile race pace, your goal should be to keep the pace of your speed runs to eight to nine minutes a mile.

The long runs would typically start at an average pace lower than your intended pace for the race, say eleven or twelve minutes a mile, and with training, you would constantly work on increasing that pace to an average of ten minutes a mile as you approached race day. Sixty to seventy percent of the runs are recovery runs, and you run at a heart rate not to exceed a target rate (180 minus your age). For example, if you are forty years old, you would try to keep your heart rate at an average of 140 beats per minute or below during your run.

Strength training focuses on building your core muscles (more commonly known as your "six pack"). You can do strength training using free weights or with your own body as the counterweight. To get my day going, one of the most useful things I did from a strength training standpoint was to incorporate "*surya namaskar*" (or "sun salutation" in English)—a series of twelve steps that include stretches and strength training using my own body as counterweight.

Cross training means giving those running muscles a break by doing alternate activities such as biking, walking, swimming, rowing, etc. I would also maximize movement by including parking my car at the farthest spot at the mall, climbing the steps at work instead of taking the elevator, etc.

While *how* you run is important, I realized early on in my running journey that *when* you run is equally important. As a rule, I tried to always squeeze my run into my mornings. If I delayed my run to a later time in the day, I was proficient at coming up with excuses to not run. I was "too tired" or "too busy" or "hurting" or some combination of the three. As I have shared before, to beat this tendency, I would have all my running gear and nutrition lined up on my dresser in our bedroom. This would remove any barriers to get going quickly in the morning. After waking up and brushing my teeth, I would put on my running clothes, do my stretches, eat or drink something quickly, put my shoes on, and go for a run right away. This kind of preparation was effective for me. Whether it is running or any other "marathons" in your life, you need to find a routine that works for you and stick to it. In our smallest routines lie the secrets of our biggest successes.

So far in this chapter, we dealt with preparing for a marathon as a runner. As I translate the discipline needed to survive and thrive in running marathons to the "marathon" of launching a startup, I find several meaningful parallels.

Let's say you have a fantastic idea to create an amazing product, service, or both that can in turn lead to the establishment of a successful startup. You have bootstrapped your company (i.e., used personal funds or those of friends and family). You have scraped the bottom of the barrel to come up with the resources including possibly taking out a line of credit against your home. You have created a minimum viable product (MVP), and it is exciting to see a product-market fit. People want your product. They *need* your product, but you must consider many factors in preparation for the gruesome "marathon" ahead. How do you get ready? One of the great books that I read on this topic was *Scaling Up* by Verne Harnish. Verne suggests that there are four key elements for success in any business, especially for startups: people, strategy, execution, and cash.

The life blood of an organization is its people. Do you have your "village" (i.e., the right combination of people assembled) with complementary talents to your own to build an incredible product or service and land your first customers? You need people with the qualified talent for sales, marketing, product, customer support, and more. Who are your superstars? How do you find and retain them? Do you have a mentor for yourself and people on your team? Do you have a backup plan if one of your superstars decides to move on? These are the fundamentals you need to work on to strengthen your "core," so you build endurance and increase your chances of success.

What is your strategy with your business? In the decades of my corporate experience across enterprises of various sizes from early-stage startups to Fortune 500 companies, I have found that there are five elements to focus on when it comes to strategy: vision, values, outcomes, RACI, and KPIs. When it comes to running a marathon, these five elements are less formalized, but they are alive and well and can help the runner succeed if these are embraced early in the journey. A similar experience awaits the startup entrepreneur embarking on his or her journey.

- *Vision* is to define your "big dream," i.e., where you are headed and what problem you are solving with your product or service.

- *Values* are what you and your team stand for that are critical as you move toward the destination.

- *Outcomes* are specific results or milestones you are planning to achieve over a specified duration.

- *RACI* stands for responsible, accountable, consulting, and informing. It defines who does what in the organization and how they work together to achieve the outcomes.

- *KPIs*—key performance indicators—are important measures of your progress defined in specific ways that are common in your industry or space.

Now let's talk about execution. This is akin to the right combination of the "practice runs" you need in preparing for a marathon. To reduce the chances of injury or failure, you will need to strengthen your "core" muscles. An example of something that I consider "core" to a startup is knowing what problem you are solving and who you are solving it for, all captured in your startup pitch. Strengthening the core in this context would mean preparing a compelling pitch well in advance and testing it with various audiences until it becomes second nature (much like core muscles would help a runner's performance). Another example is, as a runner, if I notice that I keep missing my daily runs multiple times in a week, then I pick another time of the day when I am more likely to be successful with getting those runs in. The equivalent for your startup or project might be the daily stand-ups with your team or the weekly meetings with your executive team. If you notice you are missing those opportunities to be with your team on the same page, then you need to find another time that works.

Finally, on to cash. For a startup, one of the biggest needs is the funding or free cash flow. If you are lining up funding sources, do you have a plan A, B, and C if one of the funding options doesn't pan out? If traditional sources of funding are not available, have you explored crowdfunding, SBA loans, small business grants, or local grants?

> *"By failing to prepare, you are preparing to fail."*
>
> —BENJAMIN FRANKLIN

Whether it is preparing for a marathon or building a successful startup, some common challenges may become insurmountable. We will now examine the top ten causes of failure to prepare, and then will discuss what we can do to anticipate and address each of these causes:

1. procrastination
2. self-doubt
3. access to resources
4. need for sacrifice
5. lack of expertise
6. limited support
7. risks
8. competition
9. anticipation
10. fear of failure

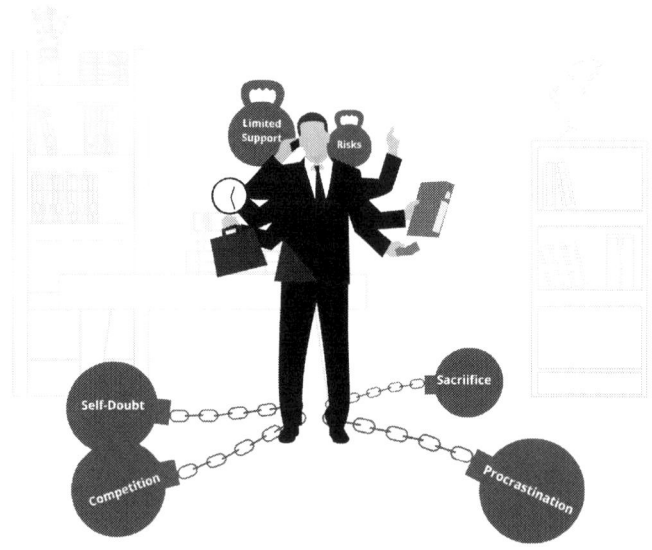

Obstacles that Hinder Preparation

Let us now highlight some of the key obstacles that hinder you from being fully prepared and then also learn how to tackle them:

- Procrastination: Procrastination is perhaps the biggest obstacle to preparation and something we all suffer from in both our personal and professional lives. Some people suffer from it more than others.

    - Examples:

        - You procrastinate the practice runs during the week and keep missing them

        - You procrastinate practicing your fundraising pitch for your startup.

- How to overcome this challenge:

    - For the weekly practice runs, I found that one of the most effective ways to address this is by scheduling the run on your calendar and getting it out of the way first thing in the morning when I have better control of my day.

    - Perfecting your fundraising pitch is going to take a *lot* of practice, and that takes time. Having done many public speaking gigs to large audiences, I am happy to share a few tips. I usually write out my speeches or presentations and try it out in front of the mirror, with friends and family, and then with professional contacts to ensure that it flows naturally. I use an accountability partner or a presentation coach if I felt I needed professional help. I then practice, practice, practice. There is no substitute for practice. The whole process typically takes three or more months if done diligently.

- Self-doubt: There were several times during my marathon journey, working for an early-stage startup, and writing this book that I experienced self-doubt or imposter syndrome.

    - Examples:

        - Was I capable of accomplishing what I had set out to achieve? And am I qualified to share insights on this topic (i.e., imposter syndrome)?

- Was I as good as the others who have accomplished the goal? These comparisons can seed self-doubt.

- When I tried something and failed, such as trying to launch a new partnership (at work) or increase my running speed (in preparation for a marathon).

- Fear of failure and embarrassment that comes from failing before.

– How to overcome this challenge and be better prepared:

- Remind yourself of the prior attempts when you thought doing something was challenging, but you succeeded anyway. For example, I reminded myself of the time that I was trying to learn "pivot tables" in Microsoft Excel and thought it was impossible. With some effort, it took only a day to figure it out. Or my initial doubts of being able to climb a fourteen-thousand-foot mountain in Colorado and succeeding in climbing twenty-six of them.

- Adopting a growth mindset as we discussed in Chapter 5: All it takes is some effort to sticking with the right mindset.

- Reminding yourself of your "why": That is the source of your motivation.

- Speaking to peers, mentors, and coaches as we discussed in the chapter "It Takes a Village."

- Access to Resources: The paucity of resources you need could be a constant challenge, whether it is a marathon journey, entrepreneurial initiative, or a sizeable project at work.

    - Examples:

        - Finding an expert in fundraising for a startup or getting better at that skill yourself.

        - Finding the information about running a marathon in Antarctica.

    - How to overcome this challenge:

        - To find an expert in fundraising or pitching, we had to look around us and our professional networks. Plenty of organizations and people are willing to help—the Founders Network, the Y Combinator, and Stanford's continuing education program. There were also tons of resources online if we wanted to get better at this ourselves.

        - By putting my request out there to my network, I was able to engage with a couple people who had run in Antarctica before. They were second- and third-level connections, but all I had to do was ask. I also found blogs and books on the topic that proved to be helpful.

- Need for sacrifice: Running a marathon takes a lot of sacrifice. Creating a new startup or working on a demanding project at work requires you to make several sacrifices.

    - Examples:

        - You might be giving up time that you could otherwise spend with the family.

        - You might have to give up a cushy steady income or benefits to create your own startup.

        - You are giving up on the luxury of sleeping in or watching TV or going out with friends.

    - How to overcome this challenge:

        - Remind yourself of your why—the goal or reason you are doing what you are doing.

        - Look at your role models, and learn from their stories of incredible sacrifices and what they were able to achieve.

- Limited Support: You will often hear empty assurances or "I am with you" when the going is good. Although I was fortunate to have had strong support from friends and family all along, I know of many people who don't have the same luxury. At the first sign of trouble or when facing a challenge, those supporters seemed to disappear.

- Examples:

    - You have encountered some challenges at work, but you are struggling with multi-tasking.

- How to overcome this challenge:

    - Don't be afraid to ask for help: Engage peers and mentors asking for specific help. Often, it may simply not be obvious that you are looking for support. Talk to friends and family about how a friend or a peer faced a challenge, and ask them specific questions about what they might be able to do if this situation were to happen to you.

- Lack of Expertise: Often, you will not be an expert at everything that you need to know when you are undertaking something new, challenging, or complex, whether it is a startup or a marathon.

    - Examples:

        - You need to fundraise or pitch for your startup, but you have no experience doing it.

        - You are preparing for a half marathon but do not have any idea of where to start or how to create a running plan.

    - How to overcome this challenge:

- First, do not use the daunting amount of work that may be involved in researching how to pitch a fundraiser as an excuse to never begin. Read books, engage experts, or take classes to learn a new skill.

- Reach out to your mentors and family to seek out experts that might know more than you do.

• Risks: Every long journey is fraught with risks. "If you risk nothing, then you risk everything," said Geena Davis (McDaniels, 2019).

  – Examples:

    - I once had to take a twenty-two-hour flight soon after I completed a race due to urgent work commitments at the startup I worked at. The risk was that I could develop deep vein thrombosis (DVT) getting on the flight before twenty-four hours had elapsed after doing a highly strenuous activity, like running the marathon.

    - You have worked for the last twelve months creating a product, but the market has moved on. You took a risk developing this product, but now you need to adapt.

  – How to overcome this challenge:

    - I decided to take this risk but mitigated it by promising myself to walk around on the plane at every opportunity and as often as I could. Thankfully, I arrived back home without incident.

- You take stock of the situation by planning for how to study the market better but also think about the future trends and adapt your changes, considering the future.

• Competition: In anything you do, someone can do it better than you. That's one way we like to think of the competition in the "traditional" sense—as another person or another company competing against you. The CEO of Netflix was asked what he considers his biggest competition. "You get a show or a movie you're really dying to watch, and you end up staying up late at night, so we actually compete with sleep," Reed Hastings said. "That's our biggest competition."

  – Examples:

    - If you are trying to secure a top spot at the marathon or within your age group or gender, then your fellow runners become your competition. Or you have competitors challenging your startup and creating disruption in the market.

    - Since you always have priorities competing for your time and preparing for a marathon takes forty to fifty hours a week, you could imagine your job or your time with friends as competition to accomplishing your marathon goals.

- How to overcome this challenge:

  ▪ You have a unique insight or skill that you continue to work on to put daylight between you and your competition.

  ▪ Recognize that you could always be doing something else, but you chose to run or dedicate your time to your entrepreneurial passion.

- Anticipation: Facing adversity and change in one's life is guaranteed. Anticipating those adversities and preparing to respond effectively enable you to handle those situations with confidence.

  - Examples:

    ▪ Blisters, cramps, or injuries ahead of or during a marathon.

    ▪ Unexpected job loss or potential to lose a major customer.

  - How to overcome this challenge:

    ▪ Blisters, cramps, and injuries are common during a marathon. Anticipate that this could happen and either work to prevent these injuries or in the case they do happen, learn how you can overcome it (especially if the injury is not life-threatening). I have learned that your mind always plays tricks on you to stop the pain. How you control your mind is up to you. More about this in the next chapter.

- We once had a major customer who threatened a lawsuit because they felt wronged with how an implementation was done by our company's professional services team. Once we did a root cause analysis of the complaint, we quickly acknowledged the issues upfront to the customer, got to the bottom of those issues rapidly, and put a plan in place around executing the changes needed and delivering on the promise of continued progress toward our commitments. It took several painstaking weeks to get this all done, and it was all hands on deck. In the end, we not only avoided the customer's lawsuit, but also made this customer into one of our most loyal customers for years. We made sure to take the lessons learned and incorporate it into our professional services team's processes going forward, so we were better prepared to avoid situations like this in the future.

- Fear of Failure: The great basketball player Kobe Bryant once said, "If you fail on Monday, the only way it's a failure is if you decide to not progress from that. To me, that's why failure does not exist. If I fail today, I'm going to learn something from that failure. I'm going to try again." What he meant was if you have not stopped trying, you have not failed. You can keep learning and persevering until you achieve the outcome you want.

- Examples:

    - Your first attempt at creating a successful startup has failed.

    - You chose a difficult race as your first marathon, and you are concerned about failing and being embarrassed. There is no way to cancel the hefty entry fees, and you have already committed to your group that you are going to run with them.

- How to address this challenge:

    - You need to learn from experience and be willing to try again and look to the future with no regrets. Remember those lessons, but focus on what you can change in the future about the outcome. Nothing more. Nothing less.

    - Once you have committed to something, there is no backing out. The optimal thing you can do is to learn about this marathon course and prepare the best you can. Talk to people who have done that run before, learn, and do what you can to anticipate and mitigate any potential challenges.

I hope this chapter has provided some valuable guidance on *why* we need to prepare, *what* obstacles may hold you back from being fully prepared, and *how* to overcome those obstacles.

It takes planning and practice, overcoming self-doubt and lots of sacrifices, seeking the right expertise and support, anticipating risks, adapting to change, and overcoming competition and failure to accomplish anything significant. Are you prepared?

Key Reflections

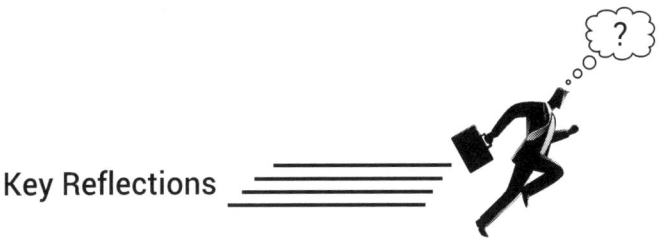

- What does it mean for you to be prepared?

- In your experience, what are the typical obstacles that come in the way of you being prepared?

- What can do you do to overcome those obstacles? Explore if any of my suggestions in this chapter can help you be better prepared.

CHAPTER 8

GRIT

---

*"Run if you can,
Walk if you must,
Crawl if you have to,
Never, never, NEVER give up!"*

—DEAN KARNAZES, AMERICAN ULTRA-MARATHON RUNNER AND AUTHOR

This is one of my favorite quotes of all time and one that comes to the top of my mind when I hear the word "grit."

As we first discussed in Chapter 2, Dr. Angela Duckworth had first introduced me to the word "grit" in a book by the same title. According to her, grit is a combination of passion and persistence to get over any kind of pain, or a combination of various strong, unpleasant feelings. The pain that you experience can be physical, emotional, or psychological; it may be temporary or even imaginary pain. Setting aside the imaginary kind of pain, your grit is what helps you get to your goal, helping you overcome the suffering along with your naysaying mind. In this chapter, we will first talk about pain, and then the grit you need to overcome it.

July 29, 2012, the San Francisco Marathon. My first marathon.

Even though I was a rookie when it came to full marathons, I found myself in one of the oh-dark-thirty running "waves" kicking off bright and early at 5:25 a.m. A little less bright. A little too early for me.

For the non-runners, a "wave" is a group of people who start together in a race, and you are placed in a specific wave based on your expected running pace and finish time. "The quicker your expected pace, the earlier your wave," the blonde-haired slim lady with the "ask me anything" badge told me sternly the prior evening when I was trying to finagle a later start while picking up my running bib at the Expo (the "bib" is that little numbered square you pin to your running outfit during the race that enables race organizers to identify you).

The previous night, with my adrenaline pumping, I barely had any shuteye. But on the morning of the race, I hardly felt sleep deprived. I figured this was due to the inner excitement and anticipation of running my first full marathon, only turbo-charged by the approximately four hundred wave mates screaming in delight and expectation. The cacophony was further amped by the thousands of runners assembled in other waves and the hordes of spectators lined up along the streets. It was not every day that you got to run on the Golden Gate Bridge. Yes, *on* the Golden Gate Bridge! It was a moment I would remember and cherish forever.

Bang! went the starter gun. And we were off! The start was awe-inspiring, the energy electrifying. I felt invincible. I was on top of the world and felt that I could run for ever. And nothing was ever going to stop me. It was a cool morning, and the sun was rising on the horizon, busy painting the sky with pinkish-red and yellowish hues. It was a stunning scene tailor-made for runners.

The first half of the marathon was energizing, even with its many ups and downs—literally and figuratively—with the natural undulations of the San Francisco landscape. Within the first two miles, I came across four people from my running group, Om Run. Having been through training with them for the past several months, we shared a unique bond, and we were now sharing a special experience.

We all smiled for the cameras, high fiving each other as the photographers feverishly looked for their next best shot. The five of us even offered the photographers creative group photos to keep things interesting. As we finished posing for pictures, a wave of runners flooded the area. They seemed to be all around us and were pushing the five of us away from each other. My eyes looked for my running mates from Om Run but, in the melee, I lost them. For a minute, I longed to have them back. But their absence was soon filled by the throngs of people standing by the road, and some were yelling, "Run, Satish, Run!" I looked to see if I would find a familiar face among the boisterous crowd, but I quickly realized they knew my name because I had it printed on the commemorative, custom running shirt I had bought the night before at the Expo.

They were calling me by different names—Saddish, Suhteeh, Sahteesh—but that did not matter. At that moment, I felt like Forrest Gump breaking free of his crutches and running away from his bullies and fears. Except here, the bullies were self-doubt, low self-esteem, and lack of confidence, and the fears were of embarrassment, injuries, and failure.

The next few miles of the race went without incident. I had made my way to mile thirteen; it was the halfway point of the race, and I was going strong. Beaming in the distance, I saw a couple of familiar faces and two young kids waving their arms, jumping up and down in sheer delight. It was my wife, Deepa, and our two children, Snigdha and Sandeep, along with my cousin, Renu. My running pace momentarily got faster, and I had a new spring in my step. They had all driven an hour from the South Bay up to San Francisco to cheer me on. I ran to them and hugged and kissed them. Barely ten to fifteen seconds later, it was time to say goodbye and keep going. I promised to see them again soon.

About twenty minutes later, I arrived at mile fifteen. I noticed the crowds had started thinning out. No more familiar faces, but I had to keep going.

As I approached mile eighteen, I felt a slight cramp in my left leg, just above the knee. *Maybe I needed more fluids and nutrition*, I told myself. I stopped at the next aid station and had my fill of Gatorade, GU gel, and protein bars. *I need to keep going. This should do it. I am already feeling better.* Or so I thought.

Barely a few minutes later, at mile twenty-two, the pain hit me like a slap across the face. Severe cramps were now in both legs. I was in so much pain that I could barely carry on. I pulled over by the side of the road, hunched over in pain, and felt that completing my first full marathon was now in jeopardy. A few minutes went by. The pain was even more excruciating!

Out of the blue, an older lady who was running by herself suddenly stopped alongside me. She mirrored my hunch and peeked at my face from below, smiled, and asked, "Are you okay, son?"

I shook my head no. "I am in a lot of pain, and I don't think I can carry on," I said.

She continued to ask questions to try to help me. She then took two salt tablets out of her runner's waist belt and suggested I gulp them down. I accepted the tablets gratefully. I had heard about salt tablets before and how the sodium in the salt could help regulate the amount of fluid in your blood and cells and that it was used often by runners to avoid cramping.

She then said, "Take one more step. Just think of your next step. Don't worry about anything else."

As she looked around to get me more help, I noticed something. On the back of her shirt was the quote attributed to Dean Karnazes that I started this chapter with. I read it again and felt a jolt of inspiration.

Take one more step, I told myself, cursing under my breath. I silently thanked this wonderful lady and Dean. Gingerly, I took one step. And one more step. I looked around but did not find the lady who had helped me. Darn. I then wished I had asked for her name as I was filled with gratitude for her. My mind wandered for a moment, and I hoped I would get to meet the great Dean Karnazes someday.

I reached mile twenty-four. My leg cramps had not gone away completely, but nothing was going to stop me. My eyes were searching again for the lady who had helped me. She was no longer with me, but she had done her part. I felt eternally grateful.

Pretty soon, the finish line emerged in sight. The screams of the throngs of people lining the sides of the marathon route had swelled and had gotten louder and cheerier. Music blared in the background, the kind of music that wants to make you dance. And run. "You can do it!" they were yelling. "You are almost there!" The photographers appeared out of nowhere and sprung back into action. You could see them everywhere now.

It is time to finish this, I muttered to myself. In the distance, I heard shrieks of joy and a few people trying to get my attention. It was my family. Seeing them, I again felt a jolt of energy running through my spine. *Just what I needed*, I told myself. I got to them and did my high-fives. My three-year-old daughter tried to cross the barrier and wanted a hug, but the race organizer volunteers didn't like that. They politely shooed her away. I understood they did this so she didn't get knocked over by other runners. Her face told me that she felt robbed of her hug, but my resolve and yearning to hug her powered me to that finish line.

It was the last mile of the race, and it felt like someone just turned on the turbo engines on my jet. This must have been one of the fastest miles of my run. Mind over matter. Perseverance over pain. And before I knew it, I had crossed the finish line. It was over. One member of the race staff jumped in front of me, putting the finishers medal around my neck. I saw a few others from my running cohort. I was elated. First full marathon. Check.

Over the course of preparing for multiple marathons in various settings across continents, I have realized that you must always *pay* with some pain and suffering as you stretch yourself to do things you have not done before. You must decide whether you *pay* with pain before or after the race. Controlled and planned pain before, uncontrolled pain and potential injuries after. Let me explain. Any pain or suffering that you experience preparing for an event is "controlled" or "planned" versus the kind of pain you experience after the event if you didn't put in the work leading up to the event. With controlled pain, you know it is coming as your body adjusts to the new challenges you are putting it through, and you can decide how much incremental suffering you want your body to endure and take action to mitigate it or reduce its impact through stretching and other techniques. If, however, you don't prepare well and don't put in work needed, you will pay for it post-race since your muscles would be overextended and your potential for injury is high. While our discussion above is about preparing for a marathon, there is a nice parallel here for preparing for a project at work.

In Chapter 1, I had mentioned that the more I ran, the more I wanted to run. Even in pain. There was something that had kept me running even through all that. Along my running journey, I started wondering what it was. Over time, I figured it out. Everyone runs for a reason, and that is your why. What is your why?

Our whys are the fuel that motivates us toward our goals, whether it is in running or an important project at work. Knowing your why helps you greatly, especially when you are faced with a challenge. My "why" may be very different from yours. Or I may even have multiple whys for a single goal. Our whys may even change over time. My why, when it came to running, started out as a challenge to myself and the self-limiting beliefs I held (and I also had that narcissistic, experienced runner to thank!). Some may run for weight loss, others for mental peace, yet others to honor someone else—a friend, a loved one, a sibling, a parent. Know your why!

Working through all those challenges and crossing the finish line at the San Francisco marathon was an important milestone in my marathon journey. I sometimes wonder what would have happened if I had stopped at mile eighteen or twenty-three and never taken another step. I am grateful for the lady who showed up like a guardian angel. I am also grateful that incident taught me something valuable. It gave me the confidence that I could work through those obstacles and emerge out of it stronger!

After the San Francisco marathon, many others followed. I remember running through a foot of water in Sacramento at the California International Marathon, running with an infected, bandaged leg in Mumbai, India, against doctor's orders (not recommended!), and running a marathon after a twenty-two-hour flight to Cape Town, South Africa, only to have to get back on a plane in fewer than twelve hours after the race due to unexpected work commitments. Was there pain? Yes. Was it insurmountable? No. Absolutely not.

I once saw a powerful phrase at my local gym plastered on the mirror in the changing room: "Pain is weakness leaving the body." With preparation, conditioning, taking meaningful risks, and putting mind over body, I found that to be the case, and it was a powerful discovery.

Now, let's talk about grit, which is what we really need when taking on any challenging project in business or life and dealing with various types of pain or obstacles.

> *"I will never quit. My nation expects me to be physically harder and mentally stronger than my enemies. If knocked down, I will get back up, every time. I will draw on every remaining ounce of strength to protect my teammates and to accomplish our mission. I am never out of the fight,"*
>
> —THE NAVY SEAL CREED QUOTED FROM THE BOOK THE LONE SURVIVOR: LOST HEROES OF SEAL TEAM 10 BY MARCUS LUTTRELL.

The Lone Survivor is an incredible, firsthand eyewitness account by Marcus Luttrell of the previously unreported, covert "Operation Redwing" in Afghanistan, led by Marcus and his team. The US Navy SEAL (SEa, Air, Land) teams are one of the most legendary, respected, and feared commando teams in the world. To become a Navy SEAL is no easy feat and requires a lot of grit. They undergo one of the most arduous training programs across the world that lasts approximately twenty-four weeks and three phases.

In his amazing book *Six Days of Impossible: Navy SEAL Hell Week—A Doctor Looks Back,* Dr. Robert Adams vividly describes the journey of a Navy SEAL. On the average, less than 20 percent of those who start successfully get through the program and go on to become official Navy SEALs. One of the most notorious and difficult parts of the program is five and a half days long, and all you get to sleep is fewer than three hours in total for the week. And what makes it worse is that it is spent in cold, wet, brutal conditions doing physically challenging training better known as "Hell Week." This week tests the physical fortitude, mental toughness, pain tolerance, teamwork, attitude, and ability to perform work under extreme physical and mental stress and sleep deprivation.

In 2012, I had the incredible opportunity to visit the Navy SEAL facility down in San Diego as part of a corporate executive training program and experienced some of Hell Week firsthand. Our general manager had decided that all seventy-six people from senior and midlevel management needed to get a taste of the mental fortitude and endurance expected of the SEALs, given the challenges we faced in tough market conditions. Our challenges obviously were nowhere close to what the Navy seals faced, of course. Getting through Hell Week is often the greatest achievement in the life of a Navy SEAL, and they leave that week with the realization that they can do much more than they ever thought possible. It is a defining moment. For many of the seventy-six of us assembled, little did we know that this was going to be a memorable moment in our life too.

When we first got to our plushy San Diego resort near the US Navy SEAL facility, we had no idea what was waiting for us. That evening, the first clue we received that something was cooking was when we saw some Navy SEALs enter the room just as we were getting ready for dinner. As a group, some whispers around the room brought up some scary possibilities. Our fearless leader Steve, with a wink and a smile, addressed the audience and promised us we would remember the next few days for forever. After a sumptuous dinner that resulted in a food-induced coma, the kind of meal I imagine people feed pigs before slaughter, Steve called the SEALs on to the stage to introduce their plans.

As part of SEAL training, the SEALs are constantly in motion—running, swimming, paddling, carrying boats on their heads—and doing physical training, which includes sit-ups, push-ups, rolling in the sand, slogging through mud, doing surf passage, and more. While describing what was in store for us, one of the SEALs said with a made-up evil, loud laugh, "Well, you are going to experience some of that. It is going to be hard, but don't worry; I assure you it is not going to be life-threatening." He added, "I promise you that." As if that made it any better.

We were to be up at 5:15 a.m. sharp and meet at a designated spot at the resort. "Don't be late, or you will regret it," the SEAL team leader said sternly. He then briefly paused and repeated, "You will all regret it even if one of you is late."

I didn't quite figure out what he meant then, but I did the next morning. The night ended with the SEALs handing out disclosure/liability waiver forms with lawyer-blessed disclaimer language, confirming that—to our knowledge—we were in good health and we didn't hold them responsible, should anything bad happen to us. That's when we knew things were going to get serious. Only those who could convince our leader Steve that they had a debilitating condition were spared. In the end, about seventy-two of us were cleared to be part of the "day from Hell Week."

The next morning, I was up by about 4:30 a.m. There was no need for an alarm clock as the Navy SEALs' words about regretting not showing up on time still echoed in my head. I jumped out of bed, took a quick shower, got in my T-shirt and shorts, and picked up something quick to eat on the way out the door. Marcus and his team were there waiting for us with big smiles and bigger voices that boomed, "Good morning!"

By 5:15 a.m., fifty-eight of us had shown up. Marcus said it was time to start with some push-ups, and we would do seventy-two of them, with an additional two push-ups each for each team member missing. We cursed those colleagues who did not show up under our breath. "We will have to make them pay later for this," I whispered to a colleague, in jest. And the Navy SEALs were barking out instructions that they wanted us to count out loud as we did those push-ups. If we were not counting in sync, we would simply have to start the count and the push-ups all over again. We became good at the counting quickly. And as some people started feeling tired, we started encouraging each other, Navy SEAL style. Teamwork and camaraderie are essential in SEAL teams as their lives depend on each other, and this bond also ensures they look out for and encourage each other to hang in there and not quit.

One of the aspects of SEAL training is that even a simple error during Hell Week could be enough for a SEAL to be disqualified or taken out of the program. And if you decide to quit or were disqualified, you were required to ring the bell. We didn't have our SEAL instructors taunting us to quit, but throughout Hell Week, instructors with bullhorns entice trainees to quit, mimicking the inner voice that tells you to give into your physical pain and suffering. The instructors made it easy, even honorable, for SEALs to come out of the cold. "Simply ring the bell that signals defeat," they would say.

As we finished our push-ups and reached the beach for the next set of exercises, what was in store for us came into view. It was a cloudy, windy day, and the waves were gloriously high. About a hundred feet away from the shore hung a huge bell. Several logs, thick ropes, and inflatable boats lay close to the water. As we approached the beach, I also noticed that an ambulance had been lurking behind us, following us slowly as an ominous reminder of what was to come.

What followed over the next two hours was perhaps one of the most brutal hours of physical activity I had ever experienced. Multiple people rang the bell and went into waiting buses where hot coffee and crispy doughnuts were beckoning them. Some of them ended up in the ambulance. The rest of us continued wincing in pain at times, pushing ropes, hauling logs, and running into the water with the inflatable boats on our heads before collapsing into them with exhaustion.

At the end of two hours, eight of us remained standing, and I was proudly one of them. The SEAL team leader congratulated us on our ability to stick with it and told us that our grit would serve us well. We were all given medals and were told we would sit at the "SEAL Honor Table" at the front of the room during dinner that night.

As I went back to the hotel and jumped into the shower, I realized I was in so much pain that I could barely lift my arms a couple feet above the resting position to wash my hair full of sand and lord-knows-what. It hurt like hell, but what an adventurous morning it had been. A salute to the SEALs and their grit! That night at the dinner, I had the great honor of meeting and spending time with some of the finest Navy SEALs including the great Marcus Luttrell, who gave me an autographed copy of his book, *The Lone Survivor*.

> "Those who completed Hell Week discovered much about themselves that most will never learn or need to know. They discovered what very few can. That the perceived impossible is possible"
>
> —DR. ROBERT ADAMS, RETIRED NAVY SEAL, DOCTOR, DELTA FORCE COMMAND SURGEON, AND AUTHOR OF SIX DAYS OF IMPOSSIBLE: NAVY SEAL HELL WEEK—A DOCTOR LOOKS BACK

Another shining and inspiring example of grit is Mahatma Gandhi, India's greatest freedom fighter against the notorious British rule. It was April 1930. The Salt March, also known as the Dandi March, was an act of nonviolent, civil disobedience in colonial India that was initiated by Gandhi to produce salt from seawater. With such a vast coastline, making their own salt from seawater was the longstanding practice of the local population. This was the case until British officials introduced steep taxation on salt production and deemed sea salt reclamation activities illegal, and then repeatedly used violent force to stop it. It was like mandating a poor man or woman earning barely a couple dollars a day to buy bottled water worth three to five dollars for their daily needs. It was an unfair and inhumane act on the part of the British.

Gandhi started the Salt March from his simple abode, the Sabarmati Ashram, near the city of Ahmedabad, India. Only seventy-eight people began the march with Gandhi, and their intention was to walk to the coastal village of Dandi. This was going to be one long walk of over 240 miles as Gandhi and the others walked to produce salt and protest the tax levied by the British. Hundreds of people came to see this frail, old man starting a movement of what would turn out to be an impressive galvanization of people around a cause. After twenty-four long days of walking more than ten miles a day, at 6:30 a.m. on April 6, 1930, Gandhi reached the shores of Dandi. The Indian Freedom struggle had begun in earnest!

Mahatma Gandhi led the fight for India's freedom for over two decades. He chose the long road of nonviolence and demonstrated true grit by repeatedly challenging the mighty British through simple acts like the Salt March. As he gripped the salt in his hand at Dandi, Gandhi inspired millions to create salt along thousands of miles of the Indian coastline. The Salt March was the spark that engaged millions of people across India to start similar acts of civil disobedience against the British, eventually resulting in India's freedom in 1947.

You might be wondering, *How do I build grit?* In *Grit*, Dr. Angela Duckworth first challenged the idea that it was talent that led to outstanding success. Through examples of students competing in the National Spelling Bee, educators working in inner city schools, or the challenges that young cadets overcome at West Point, Dr. Angela demonstrated that a special blend of passion and persistence—"grit"—is what drove success and delved into those examples to try to decipher how to build grit.

Dr. Angela explains that one can build grift in two different ways: an internal approach and an external approach. The internal approach is to develop your passion by experimenting with a variety of different things. Chances are if you are passionate about something, you are likely to be able to cope with challenges you must endure against that passion. She then suggests that with the external approach, you build grit by engaging coaches, looking up to role models, and being inspired by mentors.

To improve my running, I used a hybrid approach, leveraging both the internal and external approaches Dr. Angela proposed. I used the internal approach to experiment with different running techniques to run faster and build more endurance and settled on using aspects of "chi running." This is a technique that involves running with a strong core and a relaxed body, which reduces overuse and impact injuries. I then used a coach and leveraged mentors to further develop and change my running posture for good and getting the results I desired.

Dr. Angela also shares a great technique that can help you cultivate grit, and that technique is something you can incorporate into your daily routine. It's something that she calls the "hard thing rule." It's a ritual, where, every single day, you have to do one hard thing. The reality is that you don't grow by doing comfortable things. You get stronger by stepping outside of your comfort zone. For example, if public speaking is hard for you, then you can pick a friend or colleague you trust and practice your presentation with them. Seek their feedback and guidance on how your presentation lands with them. Then, as you get comfortable and get better at your presentation, expand your audience to try larger groups or audiences that might be new to you. "The hard thing rule" is something Dr. Angela recommends that everyone can and should incorporate into their daily lives.

In Chapter 2, we first encountered Eleanor Roosevelt's famous quote, "Do one thing every day that scares you." Ask yourself, *What can I do today that is going to challenge me?* Every day is an opportunity to perform one small act of bravery that has the potential to change the course of your life. Preparing for a marathon likely pales in comparison to the grit demonstrated by those students, teachers, and the West Point Cadets in Dr. Angela's book, the Navy SEALs, or the great Mahatma Gandhi. Still, grit is a staple need of marathon runners, entrepreneurs, students, educators, or anyone else attempting to do something that challenges them, takes them out of their comfort zone, or scares them.

As you prepare for your own "marathon" journeys, I hope these experiences and stories along with the process of building grit will serve you well.

As I heard someone once say, "Your dreams are on the other side of grit."

Key Reflections

- What is the most challenging experience you had, and how did you overcome it?

- Write down some examples of demonstration of grit that you have seen in your life.

- How would a combination of your passion and perseverance (i.e., grit) have helped you overcome that torturous experience?

- What specific actions can you take to leverage the internal and external approaches that Dr. Duckworth shared to develop your own grit?

CHAPTER 9

PROGRESS

"Impossible!" they said.

In 2012, this was the most frequent response I heard when I first shared my dream of running a full marathon across every continent. Others simply laughed at my dream—mostly in private, but sometimes to my face. They said, "Forget it! Running a full marathon is already a major challenge. And you are dreaming about running marathons across every single continent? Even Antarctica? What's next, are you going to run on the moon? Maybe Mars?" they chuckled.

I started to doubt myself. *Maybe they are right*, I thought. Running a marathon is an incredibly difficult goal, physically, mentally, and logistically. But a small part of me told me it was possible.

To fulfill my dream, I had to leverage several techniques during those dark and challenging times filled with uncertainty. Over the last few chapters, I have shared a variety of them, including the importance of showing up not just for yourself but also for others, a positive mindset, accelerating your learning using your village of mentors, coaches, and peers, why and how to prepare, dealing with pain and getting through challenging times with grit. In this chapter, we will deal with how to make progress, measure, and track it and the importance of keeping up with the progress you have made to achieve goals that may seem improbable or even impossible at first.

In Harvard business professor Teresa Amabile's book *The Progress Principle*, she talks about the importance of how making forward progress is critical to superior performance at work. She, along with her coauthor Steven J. Kramer, examined more than twelve thousand daily diaries of people working on project teams. They found that when people's perceptions, emotions, and motivations were positively influenced by the happenings around them during their workday, they performed better. And the most surprising find was that of all the things that drove positivity, one of the most critical factors was simply the feeling of making progress.

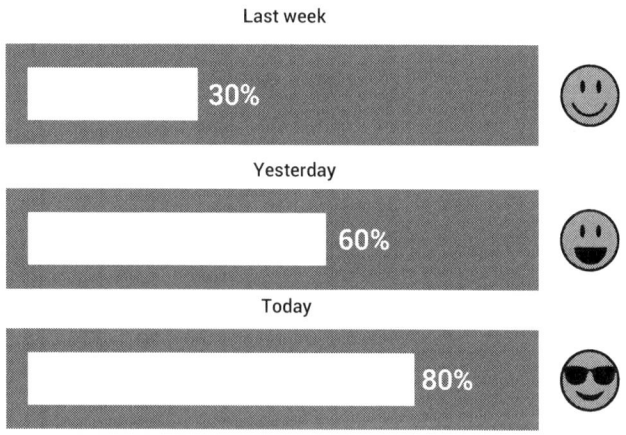

Impact of the Progress Principle

Teresa also reminds readers that even surprising little "wins" can contribute to the feeling of making progress. In my experience and the experience of so many athletes and ultra-athletes, I have found this to be so true. Travis Macy, author of *The Ultra Mindset* and one of the most admirable ultra-marathon runners who ran the Grand Prix of ultra-marathons, talks about the importance of the little wins. For example, Travis says if he is at sixty miles in a hundred-mile run, he doesn't think about the next forty miles. Instead, all he thinks about is getting to the next aid station, which may be fewer than five miles away. You may remember I had mentioned the importance of taking "one more step" when all felt lost at the San Francisco marathon. That is the "small win" I can use to relate to Teresa Amabile's findings and Travis Macy's insight.

In 2012, forget running marathons across the world; heck, I initially could not run even a few miles in my own backyard or complete a beer run. As you may recall from the introduction, this all changed when my cousin Shankar asked me if I wanted to run a couple of miles with him. And when I ran those first miles successfully, I realized I had made progress. This sense of progress created positive perceptions and emotions and motivated me to keep running. Over the next weeks and months, this progress continued in a robust fashion. Two miles turned into four, four turned into eight, eight turned into sixteen…and as they say, the rest is history.

Tracking progress is critical as we work toward our goals. To illustrate why, let's discuss an example. Imagine you are running a race. If someone in their infinite wisdom decides to remove all the mile markers along the route, what do you think will happen? Some obvious questions come up. How do the runners know the progress they have made against their goal? How do they know if they are still running along the course they were supposed to run when no signs indicating that? What happens if they veer off course? Could they get injured, dehydrated, or worse, harmed in some way? If the race is a "qualifier" for one of the major marathons (like the Boston Marathon), it could mean lost time and getting disqualified for the major race. (Note: Some of the most well-known marathons are considered "qualifiers" for highly competitive races. Essentially what this means is running at a certain pace in the race could help you qualify to run in a competitive race like the Boston Marathon.) All of this could result in massive frustration for the runners and additional liabilities for the race organizers.

This need for tracking progress is also true in the broader sense. Let's now say you are training to get ready for a marathon, which typically takes a period of four to five months. As you train, it is important to track and measure your progress so you can tell if you are getting closer to your objectives for the race. How much are you running every week? How fast are you running? What does the time of the day that you choose to run do to your running performance? What about running in a group versus alone? Does that change how you perform? As an example, I have noticed that I do best when I run in a group, early in the morning, in cooler temperatures on a light stomach, and I run faster and do better on dirt trails than on pavement runs.

Also, as you complete one marathon and start training for the next, consider how much you trained for the last one and if that felt like it was enough training. Do you need to do more or less? Do you need to reduce or increase your "taper"? For those who are new to the term taper, let me explain. Every marathon training program begins with a small number of miles, increasing the number you run every week until halfway through your program. And, as you approach the latter half of your training, you start reducing the miles as you get closer to race day (a.k.a. the taper). This is needed so you start resting your running muscles and recover in preparation for the big day!

While you may not have answers to every question listed above, it all begins with measuring and tracking your progress. When you measure, you can clearly understand what to start, stop, or continue among the various things you are doing. This applies to marathons as well as a complex work project or an idea you are launching as an entrepreneur.

As we know, it would be naïve to think things are always going to be rosy. With great progress often come setbacks. In fact, Teresa Amabile describes in her book how setbacks are sometimes two to three times more impactful than positive events in terms of progress; think of something akin to "one step forward, two steps back."

When faced with the setbacks, the motivation to keep going is both intrinsic and extrinsic in nature. For me, intrinsic motivation would be when I would remind myself that all I needed to do was to take just one more step to keep making progress. And remembering that each of those small incremental steps over time added up to many miles. The extrinsic motivation was from the mentors, coaches, and peers who reminded me that the setbacks were to be expected, and it was important to keep moving. In the end, progress was critical. And the proof is in the results measured. In the last eight years of running, I amassed nearly eight thousand miles. Have you ever told yourself something was not possible, only to be pleasantly surprised when you took just one more step?

After a successful San Francisco marathon, I felt a great sense of accomplishment about the progress I had made, and it increased my confidence that more was possible. I set my sights on the rest of the world. Several marathons followed, starting with the Prague Marathon in the Czech Republic, the Queenstown Marathon in New Zealand, the Mumbai Marathon in India, Punta Del Este Marathon in Uruguay, the Cape Town Marathon in South Africa, and the Antarctica Marathon on King George Island. Lessons were to be learned and progress was to be made in planning and execution. With some perseverance, I continued making progress with the love and support of my village. When I hit a setback, I reminded myself of the progress I had made and the need to keep going. I would like to illustrate this further with a couple examples.

The Queenstown Marathon in New Zealand was a particularly hard race with a lot of steep hills, only made harder by the sleep deprivation due to the jet lag I felt. As I ran up those hills, I felt they were more challenging than similar ones I had run before in hilly San Francisco. But then I remembered the words of my mentor to "pump your arms" when I ran up them hills. What I initially thought was criticism was sage advice that has helped me make progress up that hill in Queenstown and every other daunting hill I have climbed ever since. It is this sense of progress that was critical to keep me going.

Another example that comes to mind is running the Punta Del Este Marathon in Uruguay, South America. I remember it was a blustery, rainy, windy day. As we stood at the start line completely soaked with the wind blowing water into our faces, I remembered the progress I had made, and all I needed was to get to the first mile. As I started running the second mile, the wind kicked up, the rain got heavier. Seeing everyone around me keep going and make progress kept me going. Again, I told myself I needed to take one more step until I got to that second mile. The mantra of taking "one more step" and the feeling of making progress are what I needed to eventually get to finish line.

The final *pièce de résistance* of my marathon journey was Antarctica. I was not sure what to expect since the thought of running a marathon in the "last continent" itself was intimidating. Again, I reminded myself of the progress I had made and the "finish line" of my dream that was now in sight. I was on a ship with ninety-eight other runners, and as we approached our running destination, we heard that the weather had turned nasty the prior day and since the weather can change on a dime down there, the weather could be unpredictable the day of the marathon.

The day of the marathon turned out to be a freezing yet beautiful, sunny day. However, the sun had melted all the ice and created puddles of gooey mess all along the running track. On the first mile, my shoe got stuck in the mud and was almost swallowed by the quicksand. As I extracted the soaked shoe out of the quicksand, for a moment, I had this "sinking" feeling (pun intended), and my confidence was shaken about carrying on. I told myself all I was going to do was to put on the mud-caked, soggy shoe and take one more step. *Let's see how it goes from there after I take that step,* I remember telling myself. I took that one step and although it was hardly pleasant, it was not that bad either. True, it was a setback, but not one I couldn't overcome. I had made so much progress along my marathon journey. A wet, muddy shoe was the last thing that was going to stop me.

As we navigate challenges and crisis in our lives, I hope the lessons and insights I have shared with you will help you in your own marathons. Changing my mindset was a powerful lesson, and reaching out to the helping hands—my team of mentors, sponsors, critics, and supporters—helped me overcome any remaining obstacles.

One of my idols and favorite motivational speakers of all time, Tony Robbins, once said,

> *"In the end, what we get will never make us happy—*
> *the stars on the chart, the money we make,*
> *the number of academy awards we get.*
> *What makes us truly happy is progress.*
> *If you are not growing, you are dying.*
> *If your business is not growing, it is dying.*
> *If your relationship is not growing, it is dying.*
> *Learning and growing is critical, and making*
> *progress is an essential part of that journey."*
>
> —TONY ROBBINS

Remember the importance of progress, and when there are setbacks, start by taking one more step. The power is in the progress.

Key Reflections

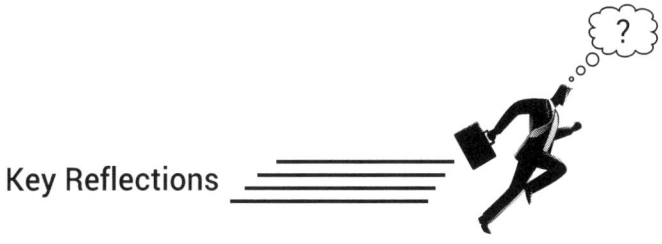

- Think of a difficult project at work you may be feeling stuck on. Have you made any progress that you can build on?

- Apply the "progress principle" and see if it may help you see any challenging project in a new light.

- If you feel stuck, think of one more step you can take to move forward. Write down that one step. Commit yourself to execute it by picking a specific time and day by when you will execute this next step. Come back here after you complete that step.

- How did completing that one more step feel? Can you think of the next step you can take? Commit yourself to execute it by picking a specific time and day by when you will execute that next step.

CHAPTER 10

AUDACITY

"Courage is not having the strength to go on; it is going on when you don't have the strength."

—THEODORE ROOSEVELT

March 20, 2019, 5:17 a.m. Somewhere near the Shetland Islands in the northeastern part of Antarctica.

I stood on the bow of the Russian icebreaker ship, Akademik Ioffe. It felt like I was in a scene from the movie *Titanic* with Jack and Rose standing on the bow, except my Rose was back home in San Jose, California.

I was alone but not lonely. I was freezing but at peace.

It was blissfully quiet except for the dull hum of Ioffe, which had dropped anchor in the bay. The constant lapping of waves at the ship's side and the sound of frolicking penguins and seals in the distance breaking through the icy waters were a sheer delight.

The silence gave me space to think, reflect, learn, and grow. I felt like I had been on an extraordinary journey that seems impossible for many. At one point, it seemed impossible for me too. Now, it seemed possible as I stood on the doorstep of running a marathon on the last continent. Only 26.2 miles stood between me and the fulfillment of my dream. Standing there, many thoughts rushed in. *Why did I even venture out on a cold, windy, icy morning? What if I slip and fall now? What if I fall sick between now and the day of the race?* For a few moments, as I played out the worst cases in my mind, the heat from all the anxiety seemed to melt the icy vastness of Antarctica that surrounded me.

The veil of darkness lifted, revealing one of the most beautiful sunrises I had ever seen. The red, orange, and blue hues heralded the impending arrival of the bright yellow ball of light, and it was a sight to behold. A part of me wondered, *Am I in a dream? Should I pinch myself?* Suddenly, a soft, muffled cry pierced the silence and jolted me back to my senses.

I looked around. Most of the people on the ship were still sound asleep after enduring two days across the "Dreaded Drake," one of the roughest bodies of water in the world. As I walked back from the bow and turned the corner, I saw a woman hunched over while she kept an eye on the horizon. She was crying silently, holding back a full-fledged bawl.

"Is everything okay?" I asked. She simply pointed to the sky, which now had changed to a broader palette of orange, pink, and blue hues as the sun was about to climb up onto the horizon.

"This is so beautiful," she said in hushed tones.

I acknowledged her, gave her the space she needed, and walked back to my place on the bow. As I turned my gaze up at the impending break of dawn, I could relate to how this beauty and peace had moved my shipmate to tears. *This is beyond beautiful. How I wish my family was here with me*, I thought to myself. *Where is a shooting star when you need one?*

A chunk of cracked ice moved away from a huge vastness in front of me and plunged into the water, which prompted my mind to go back to the memories of what I've heard about the Drake. No gentle rocking for those on the journey.

"Please tie down every untethered object in your room. We do not want any wayward flying pens, cups, books, or anything else when we get to the rough seas. And that will happen!" our team captain Jeff ordered. "Get ready to rock and roll. It is going to be a fun ride," Jeff chuckled as we set sail from the beautiful port city of Ushuaia in Southern Argentina.

We were an adventurous bunch of 120 marathoners headed to run forty-two kilometers on the "last continent" across a ten-day sojourn. "How does one achieve greatness without a little craziness?" we were asked earlier at dinner. We were shown Ernest Shackleton's ad from 1907 that apparently appeared in the *London Times*. It was believed to have been used by Shackleton to recruit courageous people for his Antarctic adventure and had ominously read, "Wanted. Men for hazardous journey. Bitter cold. Low wages. Safe return doubtful. Honor and recognition in the event of success." (Geographical Magazine, 2014). While the veracity of the ad was in doubt, much of this ad felt too real for how we felt in that present moment.

My own marathon journey across the other six continents had been through many twists and turns and ups and downs. Drake's humongous cold waves shoving us from side to side in our cabins was a stark reminder of how my own marathon journey had felt over the last seven years.

I was brought back to my senses when the voice over the loudspeaker crackled, announcing that it was time for dinner. We had had a long day since arriving in Antarctica and made our way to King George Island where we were slated to run the next day. There was a buzz around the ship about the weather being not so good that day on the island. I had almost forgotten that one of our sister ships had arrived the day before us with at least eighty more runners. And those hapless runners were slated to run their marathon that day!

Bad weather can show up in Antarctica without much warning and apparently that was what the runners faced earlier that day. As we sat down to dinner, Jeff came over the microphone, joined by Thom, the team leader from the other ship. Thom cleared his throat and, as if he was reading our minds, said, "I know some of you asked me and Jeff earlier about the rumors. Well, here I am saying they are true! But..." he paused.

No one moved a muscle in anticipation of what was to be said next. *But what, Thom?* Those words almost escaped my mouth, but I didn't utter them.

Thom sighed and smiled. "I know you are all hoping for me to say everything is going to be alright. Well, I cannot say that with any certainty!" he blurted.

My inner voice screamed, *Oh, no, that is not what we wanted to hear, Thom.*

Thom carried on. "What I can say is there will be a run tomorrow, and we will have a better day than today. And that is for certain based on the weather report as of right now." Everyone breathed a sigh of relief. You could even hear some of the claps that came through in a faint attempt at celebration. After dinner, we headed back to our bunks to try and catch some sleep.

That night was one of the longest nights of my life. I slept maybe four or five hours. I woke up at the crack of dawn and glanced through our cabin's porthole window. It was a glorious day with the sun starting to peek above the horizon. "Wow, maybe we are lucky," I said to my roommate, Rajesh. We both agreed and started getting ready. Breakfast was served, and we could hear the buzz of people outside as we ventured out of the room.

Most people were in a hurry to have breakfast as they wanted to make their way to the Zodiac boats that would take us to King George Island. Zodiac boats are like rubber dinghies but maybe ten times more robust with a strong engine fitted on one end to turbo charge your journey.

Jeff and his team had broken us up into groups, and I was among the first few groups. We were reminded to take our bottles of water—four bottles at least, food bars, and other sustenance with no wrappers. They were very strict about the "no junk left behind" rule. About thirty minutes after we left the ship, we arrived at King George Island. It was a cold yet bright, beautiful sunny day with not a hint of cloud in the sky. It was different from the dreary, cold Antarctica I had envisioned sitting in my warm backyard back in San Jose, California. As we stepped on land, it was one of those moments I could never forget. We had set foot on the seventh continent; it felt like an enormous privilege reserved for a lucky few.

As we took our first steps, there was a hint of what was in store for us that day. Remember those slushies at the 7-Eleven store in the US or Japan? A slushy is a mix of ice and God-knows-what, but it has the consistency of a rough smoothie. Well, that was what the ground was like—a bit like a slushy from the melted ice from the blizzard the previous day, mixed in with dirt and hardened snow and ice from the time of Shackleton or even older. It was hard to believe that the great Antarctic explorer and adventurer Shackleton made it that far with little to no technology or modern ice breaker ships to help him and his crew.

Despite the good weather, it was still below freezing (around thirty degrees Fahrenheit) with a light breeze blowing and negative-five-degree wind chill when we landed. I had three layers of clothing with a balaclava to protect against the cold and wind and two layers of the best winter gloves I could find. The running shoes were rated for winter conditions, water resistant, and were apparently suited for Antarctica type conditions (according to the manufacturer). For sustenance, I had three large bottles of electrolytes and a small hydration pack with me along with seven protein bars and GU gel in plastic containers.

We were to run a 4.6-mile loop six times in a row, giving us the 26.2 miles we needed to complete the marathon. Since we had a small group of staff manning the trails and we did not have formal aid stations along the route, the recommendation was to leave two bottles of electrolytes at the start of the trail and one bottle at the turnaround. That way you had access to liquids on either end of the trail, especially if you did not have a hydration pack or hydration belt with you. On the last loop, we were to pick the electrolyte bottle we had left at the turnaround when we started the race. The total elevation we had to climb was about three thousand feet, which was like climbing up about twenty Statues of Liberty. It was going to be one of the toughest races of my running adventure. But I was ready for it mentally, physically, and spiritually. After a bit of warmup runs around the island, our race was on.

We had a total of six and a half hours to complete our race, which would have been considered normal for most marathons for those who needed the extra time, but in this marathon, all bets were off as to what was considered normal. Jeff and his team had to set a time limit so they could get the race completed and wrap everything up (mile markers, banners, all-terrain vehicles, tables, chairs, and the runners had to be brought back to the ship) before the cold winds and frozen snow was expected to come in.

You may recall from the chapter on progress that when we were running our first loop out from the starting line, my shoe got stuck in the wet quicksand. The stuck shoe felt like it weighed a ton, with the quicksand around it. When I tugged at the shoe, I pulled so hard that my foot got dislodged from the shoe. For a minute, I was alarmed. But then I had seen this kind of movie many times before. I had to stay focused on what was in front of me, and nothing was going to stop me that day. Not after all the hard work and sacrifice that had gotten me to that point.

Jeff and the rest of the race organizing team had cautioned us they would be keeping an eye throughout the race for signs of dehydration, exhaustion, and more. Anyone who didn't complete roughly thirteen miles of running in about three hours would be "encouraged" to consider just finishing a half marathon, even though they had signed up for the full marathon. My time at thirteen miles was fortunately well under that threshold.

As the miles piled on, we started feeling the exhaustion creep in. The quicksand had caked on my shoe, making it heavier and extra challenging to run, but I kept telling myself I had to take "one step at a time." And that's it. As long as I kept at it, the 26.2 miles would come. And it did. I was delighted to finally cross the finish line. The organizers swooped in soon after and wanted me to go back to the boat, but I wanted to enjoy that high for a few more minutes. I walked around the island and saw the Russian church and a metal cabin that resembled a small gift shop. I entered and was pleasantly surprised to find postcards and bookmarks. I am usually not a big fan of walking into gift shops in big cities, but I was not going to pass up an opportunity to grab some collectibles from a place that was likely a "once-in-a-lifetime" visit.

As I stood on the bow of the Ioffe again on my return journey, I remember finding it hard to believe I had fulfilled my dream. And how lucky I was to have had the incredible opportunity. True, it took a lot of blood, sweat, tears, and sacrifice, but it was also a dream come true!

In the end, I was determined to not only complete this marathon successfully but to also share this message of hope and the lessons I had learned along the way to help others fulfill their dreams.

When I first set my mind on the goal of running a marathon across every continent, including Antarctica, it had seemed impossible. You may remember that some had even called it crazy then.

The Audacious Business Professional

Ultimately, with a sense of purpose, planning, discipline, a lot of grit, and most importantly, the unconditional love and support of the people around me, I was able to achieve my biggest dreams and aspirations. If I can do it, so can you. It is time to be audacious.

Carpe diem!

Key Reflections

- What is the most audacious thing you have done in your life?

- If nothing comes to mind, what is something you consider most audacious? It could be an example from work or from your personal life. It could be something you do professionally or with family or friends for fun.

- Why do you want to achieve that audacious goal (if you answer in the affirmative to one or both of the last two questions)? What do you hope to achieve (for yourself or others) by doing something audacious?

- How do you plan to achieve that audacious goal?

CHAPTER 11

FINISHING STRONG

"Life does not reward you for starting. Only finishing."

—GARY RYAN BLAIR

You either finish or you do not. It's that simple. After having run nearly eight thousand miles over eight years, it is clear to me that the battle to finish and finishing strong is won or lost between your ears. In other words, it is all about your mindset.

Gary Ryan Blair reminds us there are no rewards for starting—only finishing. The very nature of finishing every day, every race, every project in a strong fashion demonstrates your commitment and sets us up for practicing mental toughness. This toughness in turn creates a psychological edge that enables us to remain focused and confident during high-pressure situations to perform to our full potential and finish what we started. The ultimate measure of mental toughness is consistency. Your ability to rise to every challenge, to bulldoze your way through any resistant forces, and to consistently finish strong will be what sets you apart from those who want to achieve great things (Blair, 2018).

One of my mentors once shared this powerful quote:

"If you make a commitment, honor it. If you make a promise, keep it. If you set a goal, achieve it."

WHY FINISH?

In this section, we will explore why it is important to finish anything you start.

BUILDS DISCIPLINE

Finishing anything you start takes putting into practice several principles, despite how you feel at the time. These principles include knowing your why, having the right mindset, breaking down goals into smaller or more meaningful milestones, building grit and resilience, and working through pain and obstacles. Finishing strong builds the discipline we all need when we face obstacles, which we will invariably encounter. When you are committed to completing something, you may need to experience pain and sacrifice, but with the commitment overriding everything else, you are bound to build the discipline you need.

Growing up in a strict home, I remember my dad waking up every day at 5:30 a.m. even if we were up late the previous night. After waking up, he would make coffee for the household, prepare the ingredients for breakfast to help my mom, and get ready for work. He would then wake up my mom, and by the time he got to our bedrooms to wake us up, I usually was already awake. I enjoyed waking up and having a fresh, hot cup of coffee in a relatively quiet house. Watching my dad do this every single day created the discipline in me to be the early riser, and to this day, I wake up early, whether it is a weekday or the weekend. This flabbergasts my well-meaning wife, Deepa, who wants me to sleep in occasionally, but I am a creature of habit.

REVEALS CHARACTER

Finishing strong builds character since it is when the body is exhausted, the energy is depleted, and the will is diminished that your true character is revealed. Your mind starts to play games with you. Your body is screaming for you to stop! What you do then is ultimately what matters and enables you to finish strong.

I have mentioned the euphoria I felt when I started running a marathon. You feel like you are on top of the world. You feel you can run forever. But then as the race goes on, you start feeling pain and your body screams for you to stop. When you don't finish, you are not keeping a commitment to yourself.

Growing up, my mom always exhorted me to finish what I started. She said it reveals character. She would say, "Deep down, a person has something special in them that makes them keep their commitment to get themselves across their goal line every time." It is something I have worked on ever since. I have tried to incorporate this mindset into my running, at work, and most other areas of the life. I have had challenges in multiple marathons especially when I had to travel to the other side of the globe, run the race while still jetlagged, and complete what I started successfully. In my work, there are times when I had to work very long hours or into the weekend to keep a commitment I made to my team or my manager. In my mind, there is no alternative but to keep that commitment and finish what I start.

CREATES EXPECTATIONS
By making a habit of finishing anything you start, you are setting expectations for yourself. These expectations will not let you accept anything less than finishing, even if it takes you longer or you must work harder to get it done.

When I encountered the challenge of my shoe disappearing in the slushy quicksand during the first mile of my Antarctica Marathon, I had set the expectation for myself that I needed to extract the shoe and keep moving. This expectation helped me overcome any distractions caused by the fully soaked shoe and is one of the key factors of my ability to keep going and finish that race.

FOSTERS CONFIDENCE
When you consistently finish and finish strong, it fosters the confidence that you can get something done. When I was running my marathon across my fifth continent in Mumbai

with an injured leg, I had already gained the confidence that I was going to finish the race, come what may. Having finished the past marathons successfully and having trained for the race itself and building the discipline fostered that high level of confidence in me.

BUILDING THE CAPACITY TO FINISH STRONG

Now, we will explore how to build the capacity to finish strong.

KNOW YOUR PURPOSE

You may have heard someone say, "It is purpose that got me out of bed every morning." Well, it is purpose or your intention that really helps you fuel your ability to finish. The more meaningful your purpose is to you, the greater your ability to finish. An example to illustrate this further may help. Say your family is on a road trip to a destination that is hundreds of miles away, and halfway through that trip, you get a flat tire. Your purpose is clear: to get you and your family to that destination safely and make it an enjoyable road trip for you and them, and you are not going to let anything stop you. You will do your best to fix that flat tire or call for help as soon as possible. The purpose of getting to that destination (and finishing this trip) will be fueled by your purpose to get you and your family to your destination safely without causing too much stress for them.

BREAK IT DOWN

One reason many never make it to the finish line is they are overwhelmed by their big goal. By breaking down the goal into intermediate milestones, you are more likely to cross that finish line for those intermediate goals. You can then work your way toward crossing the finish line of your next, bigger goal. Before I got to the start line of my full marathon, I ran a 5K, 10K, half marathon, and then—and only then—did I go on to run my full marathon. I know so many people who have "run a marathon" on their bucket list. They start enthusiastically, but a few weeks in, they start feeling overwhelmed with it all. They procrastinate and become stagnant. This stagnation eventually leads to them abandoning their goal.

FOCUS ON PROGRESS

During my marathons, I would always focus on getting to the next mile. In fact, as things got tougher (as they often did, especially toward the end of the race), I would just focus on taking the *next step*. This is what ultimately got me across the finish line in San Francisco.

Many endurance athletes talk about focusing on being present and the power of focusing on incremental progress to successfully get them across the finish line. The Marathon des Sables, or MdS, is a six-day, 251-kilometer (or 156-mile) ultra-marathon, which is approximately the distance of six regular marathons. The longest single stage is ninety-one kilometers (or fifty-six miles) long. This multi-day race is held every year in southern Morocco in the Sahara Desert. It has been regarded as the toughest foot race on Earth.

Josef Ajram, Spain's top endurance athlete, has completed the Marathon de Sables by only allowing himself to think about the next fifteen minutes: "I will run another 15 minutes. Come on. Anyone can run another 15 minutes."

Josef says this is the secret to his success and finishing strong. If Josef Ajram can repeat these words and find them a great source of motivation to finish such a stunning feat and to stay on top as a top endurance athlete, we can all find our own motivation to finish too.

PRACTICE VOLUNTARY HARDSHIP
The concept of "voluntary hardship" is to build discipline by constantly doing something that takes us outside our comfort zone and hardening ourselves, preparing us for the day we must face the discomfort for real. We discussed this concept also on the chapter on grit.

In running, I practiced voluntary hardship by doing things that were uncomfortable for me. Doing a sprint at the end of my run when I was the most exhausted or running a bit longer, faster, or harder during a long run are examples. In other areas of life, getting out of bed when the alarm sounds no matter how groggy you feel or how much you want to stay in bed, doing an intermittent fast even if you don't have to diet, subjecting your body to slightly more extreme temperatures (cold or hot), choosing to walk up a steep hill (instead of a flat trail or road), and doing it better every time are examples of voluntary hardship.

As an entrepreneur, working those extra hours at the end of the day or over weekends to build a better product or to prepare for a pitch or to build a new skill that is not part of your repertoire are examples of voluntary hardship. Our ability to constantly test ourselves and keep going when it is uncomfortable is a testament to building discipline and being able to finish strong when we encounter some of these challenges.

In this chapter, we have examined what it means to finish strong, why it is important to do so, and the various techniques you can leverage to build the capability to finish strong.

In the words of the famous author Robin Sharma,

"Starting strong is good. Finishing strong is epic!"

—ROBIN SHARMA

Wishing you an epic finish.

Key Reflections

- Have you ever struggled with finishing what you started? Are there certain types of tasks you struggle to finish?

- How often do you struggle with finishing? Have you diagnosed what the challenge(s) you have with finishing are? What have you done so far to address and overcome those challenges?

- Have you tried using any of these techniques with overcoming the challenges to finish something you start—knowing your purpose, breaking it down, focusing on progress, voluntary hardship? Pick one or more, and give it a shot.

Do you have other techniques that have worked for you? What are they? Write to me at https://satishshenoy.com/contact-me/ and let me know!

PART 3

APPLYING THE PRINCIPLES

CHAPTER 12

AFTERWORD

"Dream your own dreams, achieve your own goals. Your journey is your own and unique."

—ROY T. BENNETT

What a journey it has been!

Living through the "marathon" adventure across the seven continents and having the privilege of sharing that adventure with you through this book has been a great honor. My heartfelt gratitude to you for giving me this opportunity. I hope it has been as fun for you as a reader as it has been for me writing this book.

The best journeys answer the questions that, in the beginning, you didn't even think to ask. We all know the trek of 26.2 miles or even a thousand miles begins with a single step. Keep taking that next step.

Wishing you incredible success in your own life's "marathons."

See you on the trails, wherever they may be.

CHAPTER 13

A COLLECTION OF KEY REFLECTIONS

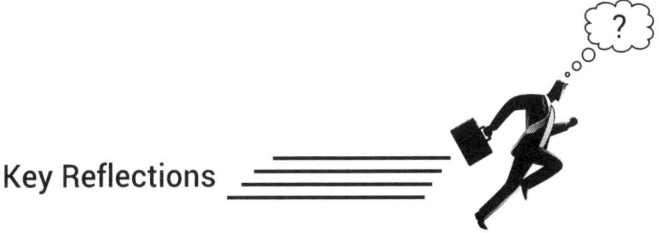

> *"Without execution, 'vision' is just another word for hallucination."*
>
> —MARK V. HURD, EX-CEO, HEWLETT PACKARD

INTRODUCTION
This book introduces a framework and key principles to achieve extraordinary goals and fulfill your big dreams. These goals may span your business life including moonshot

projects at work, an idea you are trying to bring to life with your startup, your next run or sports activity, or something else you deem important.

Over the course of the chapters in this book, I have been excited to share what I have learned from my own experience and others that inspired me along that journey. I hope these stories and lessons invigorate you to go after your big dreams, get into the right mindset, create your own village, overcome pain and demonstrate grit, and keep taking one more step to get you to your goal.

However, all that sharing is for naught if you cannot relate this back to your own life and implement the framework and principles I share in this book. That is why I introduced "key reflections" at the end of each chapter throughout the book.

I hope you have been reflecting upon all you have learned as you went through this book. In this chapter, I have brought together all key reflections for your convenience and continued learning to help you achieve your big dream.

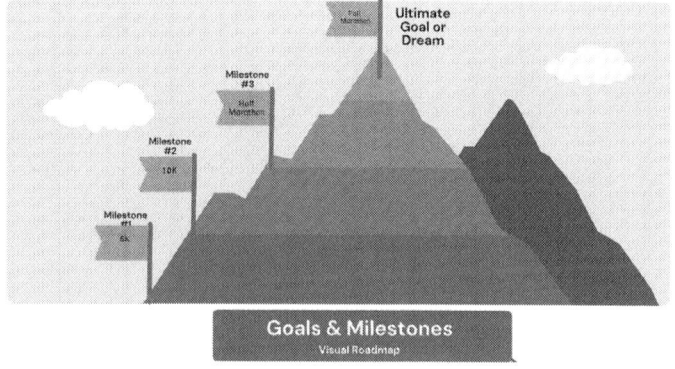

CHAPTER 2: YOUR VISION, GOALS, AND BIG DREAM

- What is/are your big dream(s)?

- Why do you have these big dream(s)? What led you to it?

- What has been your biggest fear or obstacle in achieving this big dream?

- What smaller, achievable, measurable goals can you set for yourself to fulfill your big dream?

- Leveraging the five-step framework, write down the relevant steps that surround your big dream and the activities and the outcomes you plan for at each step.

CHAPTER 3: REACHING HIGHER

- Write down one (or more) goal(s) that scare you.

- Write down three things you will be willing to attempt as a goal (these could include things you have never attempted before or attempted and failed).

- What is something that makes you feel like an imposter? Why does it make you feel like an imposter? Is there anything you could do to overcome that feeling?

CHAPTER 4: SHOWING UP

- What does it mean for you to "show up"?

- Pick an activity and write down specifically how you will prepare to show up.

- If it is an activity that requires *consistently* showing up, how are you going to hold yourself accountable to keep showing up the way you want to every time?

_____

_____

_____

_____

THE SEVEN PRINCIPLES

In this book, I have shared several of the principles that worked for me to achieve seemingly impossible or even improbable goals. Which of those principles resonated with you? Why? How do you hope to use that in achieving your big goal or dream?

- **Mindset**
- **It Takes a Village**
- **Preparation**
- **Grit**
- **Progress**
- **Audacity**
- **Finishing Strong**

PRINCIPLE ONE: MINDSET

- Would you say you have a fixed or growth mindset? Think about specific examples and why you think so!

- What is an activity or goal that you have felt was outside your realm of achievement? Apply the three-stage mindset tool and explore where you are in that journey.

- If you are stuck on either step one or two of the three-stage mindset transformation, what can you do to get to the next stage?

_____

_____

_____

_____

PRINCIPLE TWO: IT TAKES A VILLAGE

- Have you had a mentor or a coach in your life? What impact have they had?

- Was the mentor a cheerleader, a sponsor, or a critic? Have you had multiple mentors at one time?

- Write down three active mentors and three passive mentors in your life. Share the areas of your life they impacted.

- Have you created your own village or community? Are you part of someone else's village?

- Do you have all three important elements in your village or someone else's village that you are part of—namely mentors, coaches, and peers?

PRINCIPLE THREE: PREPARATION

- What does it mean for you to be prepared?

- In your experience, what are the typical obstacles that come in the way of you being prepared?

- What can do you do to overcome those obstacles? Explore if any of my suggestions in this chapter can help you be better prepared.

PRINCIPLE FOUR: GRIT

- What is the most challenging experience you had, and how did you overcome it?

- Write down some examples of demonstration of grit that you have seen in your life.

- How would a combination of your passion and perseverance (i.e., grit) have helped you overcome that torturous experience?

- What specific actions can you take to leverage the internal and external approaches that Dr. Duckworth shared to develop your own grit?

PRINCIPLE FIVE: PROGRESS

- Think of a difficult project at work that you may be feeling stuck on. Have you made any progress that you can build on?

- Apply the "progress principle" and see if it may help you see any challenging project in a new light.

- If you feel stuck, think of one more steps you can take to move forward. Write down that one step. Commit yourself to execute it by picking a specific time and day by when you will execute this next step. Come back here after you complete that step.

- How did completing that one more step feel? Can you think of the next step you can take? Like what you did before, commit yourself to execute it by picking a specific time and day by when you will execute that next step.

PRINCIPLE SIX: AUDACITY

- What is the most audacious thing you have done in your life?

- If nothing comes to mind, what is something you consider most audacious? It could be an example from work or from your personal life. It could be something you do professionally or with family or friends for fun.

- Why do you want to achieve that audacious goal (if you answer in the affirmative to one or both of the last two questions)? What do you hope to achieve (for yourself or others) by doing something audacious?

- How do you plan to achieve that audacious goal?

_____

_____

_____

_____

PRINCIPLE SEVEN: FINISHING STRONG

- Have you ever struggled with finishing what you started? Are there certain types of tasks/projects you struggle to finish?

- How often do you struggle with finishing? Have you diagnosed what the challenge(s) you have with finishing are? What have you done so far to address and overcome those challenges?

- Have you tried using any of these techniques with overcoming the challenges to finish something you start—knowing your purpose, breaking it down, focusing on progress, voluntary hardship? Pick one or more, and give it a shot.

Do you have other techniques that have worked for you? What are they? Write to me at https://satishshenoy.com/contact-me/ and let me know!

WHAT'S NEXT

Have you fulfilled your big goal or dream or at least made substantial progress toward fulfilling your big dream? If not, you know I am counting on you to finish. Keep at it. Take one more step and keep taking one more step. Before you know it, you will be there.

If you have finished, heartiest congratulations! And keep reading...

Now that you have finished your big goal or dream, reflect on what else you can do. When I finished my first marathon, I reflected on it and decided to run more marathons. My calling was when I read about the Seven-Marathon Club and wanted to be part of that club by running at least one marathon across all seven continents. I also wanted to share what I had learned with young kids and get them into running. I trained a group of kids four to fourteen years old for several years; I started with a group of five kids, and in the third year, the group swelled up to fifty-three kids.

Can you share what you learned? Can you teach someone? Speak about it? Write about it? (So many options are available these days—blogs, *Medium*, etc.) Maybe a podcast? YouTube Video? A book?

The options are limitless, and the world is your oyster. Write it all down, and go make it happen! May the force be with you.

*"Starting Strong? Good.
Finishing Strong? Epic!"*

— ROBIN SHARMA, MOTIVATIONAL AUTHOR & SPEAKER

ONLINE RESOURCES

As a reminder, for an additional set of resources, including free downloads of practical tools, intriguing insights, inspiring quotes, interesting pictures of my journey, and more, please join me online at https://satishshenoy.com/author/ or scan this QR code to be taken directly to my page:

CHAPTER 14

THE SEVEN-CONTINENT ADVENTURE: A PHOTO JOURNEY

---

*"A good snapshot keeps a moment
from running away."*

—E. WELTY.

After my seven-continent running adventure, I observed that whenever I shared pictures of the various places I had been, I received positive feedback, and it seemed to enhance the experience of the person hearing the story. This was especially true for a place like Antarctica, which feels like a "once-in-a-lifetime" experience. And then there are places considered exotic or mysterious, like far-flung Africa, South America, or India.

So, firstly, I feel fortunate to have been on this incredible journey and am delighted to share these pictures in the hopes that it enhances your experience.

Secondly, I share these pictures because they can sometimes convey what words struggle to describe eloquently. As they say, "A picture is worth a thousand words."

Finally, there is the adage, "Seeing is believing." By seeing these pictures, it hopefully "authenticates" the experience for you, the reader, and helps educate you further like it did for me.

What follows in this chapter is a set of twenty-three pictures I chose to share with you. These are pictures from each of the marathons I ran across the world. These pictures hopefully help you vicariously live this journey with me and enhance your overall experience as these pictures support the stories I tell in the book.

Enjoy!

The Seven-Continent Marathon Adventure

Getting acclimatized in Buenos Aires

In Ushuaia, the world's southernmost city

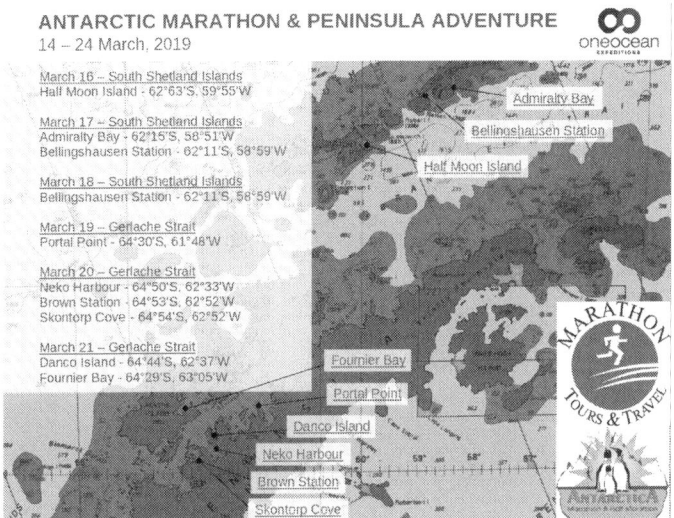

Charting our fourteen-day journey

The Russian Icebreaker Akademik Ioffe

Settling into our cabin on the Ioffe

Ioffe in the Drake Passage

One in a million: penguins in Antarctica

Heading to King George Island using specialized boats called the Zodiac

THE SEVEN-CONTINENT ADVENTURE: A PHOTO JOURNEY · **185**

A gorgeous day for a run in Antarctica

Watch out for penguins!

The shoes tell the story

Post-race Antarctica version of an ice bath

Hanging out with a curious friend

My first taste of a half marathon: The Oakland Half

The San Francisco Marathon: What a roller coaster!

My personal cheering squad in San Francisco

Conquering the cobblestone streets of the Prague Marathon

My awesome support team in Prague

In the City of Dreams, Mumbai

Getting to know the Land of The Lord of the Rings, New Zealand

In Punta Del Este, Uruguay

Running in the lap of the mother city, Cape Town, South Africa

ACKNOWLEDGMENTS

"If the only prayer you said was thank you, that would be enough."

—MEISTER ECKHART

Although a marathon is viewed as an individual sport, crossing the finish line successfully is only possible with the unconditional support of a team of family, friends, peers, mentors, and coaches over an extended period; an author's journey is similar. Writing a book is truly a "marathon" journey, maybe even more so than running the marathon itself. For those on the outside, the author's journey may feel like an individual "sport," but I can tell you from my personal experience that an author is only successful due to the efforts, help, and sacrifices of family, friends, acquaintances, peers, mentors, coaches, and a great team of editors, marketers, and fellow authors who surround him or her over a duration that lasts a year or more.

The sentiment of "never giving up" first came from my dad, Sadananda Shenoy, and my mom, Sudha S. Shenoy, who were there (at least virtually) to see me cross the finish line of my marathons, but both passed on peacefully during the creation of this book. They will forever be part of who I am and what I have accomplished. I owe them a deep sense of gratitude that is hard to put down in words.

I feel incredibly blessed to have such an amazing family and an extraordinary group of friends. First and foremost, I feel lucky to have a truly wonderful life partner in my wife, Deepa, and my children, Snigdha and Sandeep. Deepa, Snigdha, and Sandeep not only encouraged me throughout my running marathon journey, but also continued that support during the author journey, which felt like an even bigger marathon. I often missed movies, dinners, and just hanging out with the family due to my responsibilities as an author, and they simply understood that I needed to get things done. Deepa helped me through multiple book revisions, supported my family's needs as I dedicated time to the book, and just kept me going until it was done. Snigdha and Sandeep wrote their first book *Public Speaking for Kids* (https://boldspeaker.com/) in the fall of 2020 even as the pandemic raged, and that became an inspiration for me and pushed me to get things going on my own writing aspirations.

My sincere gratitude to several members of my extended family, especially my brother, Sudhir Shenoy, who not only helped me during my book campaign, but also spread the word of my campaign to line up support to my campaign from even far-flung Singapore where he lived. My brothers Sudarshan and Suresh taught me valuable life lessons as all older siblings do, for which I am grateful. To my cousin, Anandi Shenoi, who generously gave to my campaign and was one of the first to step up to be a beta reader. And to my other cousins, Anita and Manohar Shenoy, and their spouses, Suresh and Gowri, who also generously supported me during my campaign.

Thank you also to my in-laws, Rathanker and Savithri Shanbhogue, who have been like my parents were to me, constantly guiding, providing support, and sharing their wisdom. My gratitude to my sister-in-law and her husband, Roopa and Shivananda Prabhu, and their wonderful children, Siddharth and Bumika, who were ardent supporters of my marathons and have been of my author journey also. I still remember how Roopa even nursed a wound on my leg for several days leading up to the Mumbai marathon, and Shivananda, who arrived near the finish line with the family and ran the last portion of the Mumbai marathon on the sidewalk just to cheer me on and help me complete the race. Another person I cannot forget who helped me ahead of the Mumbai marathon was Shobha Mayee, a neighbor next door in Mangalore. She cared for me for about ten days during my stay there prior to the race, healing my leg wound considerably before Roopa took over.

To Rajesh Setty, who has not only been my mentor but a friend who is more like a brother to me. He first lit that spark in me to write this book and was the one who brainstormed with me to come up with the working title *Run and Grow Rich* and then jumped in again when the title evolved to *Runaway Growth*. He gave me access to his course "The Right Hustle" freely (which is an amazing resource for anyone) and Audvisor subscriptions at cost to help me energize my campaign. His wisdom, his insights, his kindness, and his generosity are beyond compare.

A big thanks to a number of these folks who not only championed my book campaign but also read my manuscript and offered me valuable feedback: Nathan Gold, Rita Barber, VP Shenoy, Anandi Shenoy, Mahesh Narasimhan, Ranga Ranganathan, Prasana Iyengar, Rajesh Bharatiya, Deepa Shenoy, Helen Keenan (who, with her husband, Bruce, also helped make connections to a great runner after reading my story), and Dr. Robert Adams. In the end, your feedback on the book is what made this book that much better.

I am immensely grateful to Professor Koester of the Creator Institute at Georgetown University and Brian Bies, head of New Degree Press. I am thankful to my developmental editor, Benay Stein, who worked with me tirelessly to help me build the foundation for this book. Thanks also to my acquiring editor Lauren Sweeney for the detailed feedback and showing me how to implement that feedback. To my marketing and revisions editor (MRE), Mozelle Jordan, and the MRE wrangler, Kristy, who worked with me through my personal ups and downs throughout my successful book campaign and multiple revisions to get me to the finish line. To my author coaches, especially John Saunders, Kyra Ann Dawkins, Mackenzie Finklea, S. D. Howard, Emily Vanderbilt, and everyone else who shared incredible insights in a timely fashion and who were always open for a conversation and worked hard to assist us authors at NDP. I am grateful to my fellow authors with whom I have become great friends, starting with Bailey Li, Nancy Smith, Melissa Carr, Sherice Shine-Cross, Snigdha Nandipati, Dilip Ramachandran, Precious McKoy, Dr. LaNysha Adams, Somer Hackley, Moshe Goldstein, and others I met through the Creator Institute and NDP. Thanks also to Thom Gilligan from Marathon Tours and

Travel (which is a phenomenal organization for supporting runners' adventures around the globe), Marathonphotos.live, Marathon Foto, and Marcio Rodriguez from Foco Radical for explicitly endorsing the use of photos and other related material in this book I had bought from them or received in using their service.

To my coconspirator in marketing, Joshua Rozario from Mindshare Digital Inc.—the brainstorming, the late nights, the unique ideas, the insights he brought, all the encouragement, and the backing he offered are beyond what I had expected. Thanks also to his family who put up with my requests, sometimes at the most inopportune times of the day or night. And to Meenakshi Kodati—in recognition of her collaboration and responsiveness, the brilliance of some of her designs, and her hard work in support of my marketing campaigns and related efforts.

To Patrick Finn, the general manager of the Americas business at the technology company I work at—he took a deep interest in my book, understood, and admired the effort I was putting in, gave me access to the virtual stage to introduce my book to fellow leaders at the company, and was among the first to support my book campaign. He then so generously introduced me to General John Sattler (Retd.) when I approached him with a request to introduce me to any military leaders he knew and admired so I could interview them for the book. Pat is an incredible leader with an uncanny sense of intuition picking up on the smallest of challenges faced by members of his team, has the generosity of heart and spirit, and is among the rare set of business leaders I will follow into battle any day.

To Linda Dotts—a thoughtful, empathetic, and respected leader I have learned from in almost every interaction I have with her. I first met Linda almost a couple decades ago when I was in Singapore and she took on the general manager role of a struggling business in Japan, for a large telecom company we both worked for at the time. The fact that she led and turned around a significant business and grew it against many odds in a male-dominated, xenophobic society was both impressive and invigorating. From the very beginning, her quiet, balanced, yet highly influential style of leadership, challenging the norms, and leading by example have all been awe-inspiring. Thank you, Linda, for all you have done for many and the support and mentoring you have offered me in my professional life as well on this book journey.

To the early backers of my book campaign—you invested in me, and that says a lot about your belief in me. Ajay Kapoor, Albert Pessot, Alisa DiStaso, Alisa M. Parenti, Anandi Sujeer, Anita Rao, Anitha Kannan, Ashraf Yussouff, Bailey Li, Balachandar Naidu, Bella Toomey, Benjamin Lingard, Bharat Gupta, Bhavesh Davda, Brad Hairston, Bruce Mazza, Catherine Gatus, Chandra Ravipati, Chinmaya Gogineni, Chitra Madhwacharyula, Dr. Michael Cocchini, Dan Waldschmidt, Daniel Rachlin, Declan Shalvey, Denise McMahon, Dilip Ramachandran, Dionis Rodriguez, Dolly Menashe, Doug Peris, EeLin Golan, Eric Koester, Eugene Sullivan, Gavin Wang, Gemma Brown, Girish & Sangita Prabhu, Glen D. Smith and Robert Casey, Harbinder Khera, Harry Saint-Preux, Helen Keenan, Iyad Uakoub, Jack Ross, Jay Mojnidar, Jayesh & Ritu Goyal, Jenny Rush, Jondi-lee Jodi Gray, Joshua Rozario, Joy Francis, Jitender Singh, Julie Hart, Karen Cornwell, Kiran Sirupa, Dr. LaNysha Adams, Lauri Kay Elbing, Lee McKillip, Leor Grebler, Lexie Smith Yanping Li, Linda Dotts,

Lori Moss, Luna Gladman Michael Nixon, Mahesh and Shailaja Narasimhan, Mandy Robertson, Manish & Nikita Krishnan, Manohar & Gowri Shenoy, Mario De Croos, Megan Mayer, Michael & Rafaela Gittens, Mohan & Vanita Chandrashekar, Mohan Gote, Moshe Goldstein, Muneyb Minhazuddin, Nathan Gold, Nick Adams, Nilesh Patel, Parag & Preethi Bhatt, Paul Nerger, Pavan Datla, Pawan Jadhav, Patrick Finn, Phalguna Rao, Pradyut Bafna, Prasana Iyengar, Praveen Mamnani, Premtim Dervishaj, Rachita Sundar, Rafael Chac, Rajbir S Chahal, Ranga and Madhu Ranganathan, Ram & Padma Alluri, Ram Valliyappan, Ramesh Panuganty, Ravi Parthasarathy, Revathi Iyer, Rita Barber, Roopa and Shivananda Prabhu, Ron Raczkowski, Ryan Tetreault, Santhosh and Saritha Rao, Satyan Shah, Saurabh Kumar, Scott Spaulding, Sesha Shayan Nandyal, Shailesh Kumar Verma, Shameela Jalari, Shaun Trejo, Sherice Shine-Cross, Snigdha Nandipati, Sowmya Gottipati, Srividhya Venkat. Stephanie Musal, Steve Abraham, Steve Marconi, Steve Regini, Subramanyam Dravida, Sudharsan & Usha Rangaswamy, Sudhir Shenoy, Sumit Sood, Tarun Raman, Trevor Duguay, VP Shenoy, Venkat Vijayraghavan, Venkatakrishnan Raman, Venkatesh Iyengar, Victor Ramirez, Vijay Jagannath. Vladimir Petkov, Wendy Bohling—a big thank you.

And finally, I would like to express my deepest gratitude to you, my readers, who ultimately this book is all about. This quote says it better than I ever could.

> *"When eating fruit, remember the one who planted the tree."*
>
> —VIETNAMESE PROVERB

While this book is a fruit of my labor and of all the great contributions from many along the way, it is you, the reader, who planted the tree. For that, I am eternally grateful.

Thank you for making it all possible.

APPENDIX

CHAPTER 1: INTRODUCTION

Galloway, Jeff. *The Run-Walk-Run Method*. Aachen, Germany: Meyer & Meyer Sport, 2016.

Stiller, Ben, dir. *The Secret Life of Walter Mitty*. Los Angeles, CA: Twentieth Century Fox, 2013.

CHAPTER 2: SMALL GOALS, BIG DREAMS

Duckworth, Angela. *Grit: The Power of Passion and Perseverance*. New York, NY: Simon & Schuster, 2016.

King, Martin L. "I Have a Dream." Speech presented at the March on Washington for Jobs and Freedom, Washington, DC, August 1968.
https://avalon.law.yale.edu/20th_century/mlk01.asp.

King, Martin L. "7 Achievements of Martin Luther King Jr." World History Edu. June 2019.
https://www.worldhistoryedu.com/martin-luther-king-jr-achievements/.

Lucas, George, dir. *Star Wars*. San Fransico, CA: Lucasfilms, 1999.

Pink, Daniel. "Dan Pink on Why Projects Need a Premortem." Facebook. Video, 1:54. May 29, 2018. https://www.facebook.com/watch/?v=249989855562693.

Rowling, J. K. *Harry Potter Series*. New York, NY: Scholastic Press, 1998.

Samuelson, Joan Benoit. "Goal Setting." Masterclass. Video, 10:20. January 2022. https://www.masterclass.com/classes/joan-benoit-samuelson-teaches-the-runner-s-mindset/chapters/goal-setting.

CHAPTER 3: REACHING HIGHER

Encyclopedia Britannica Online. Academic ed. s.v. "altitude sickness." Edited September 26, 2021. https://www.britannica.com/science/altitude-sickness.

Pakula, Alan J, dir. *Sophie's Choice*. Universal City, CA: Universal Pictures, 1982.

CHAPTER 4: SHOWING UP

Cicero MT, and Younge CD (translator). 46 BC (1877). Cicero's Tusculan Disputations. Project Gutenberg.

Pinola, Melanie. "Inspiration Is for Amateurs—The Rest of Us Just Show Up and Get to Work." Lifehacker. March 1, 2013. https://lifehacker.com/inspiration-is-for-amateurs-the-rest-of-us-just-show-u-5972825.

Weiner, Eric. *The Socrates Express.* New York, NY: Avid Reader Press / Simon & Schuster, 2020.

CHAPTER 5: MINDSET

Dweck, Carol S. *Mindset.* New York, NY: Ballantine Books, 2006.

Gandhi, Mahtma. "Quotable Quotes." Goodreads. Accessed on March 10, 2022. https://www.goodreads.com/quotes/50584-your-beliefs-become-your-thoughts-your-thoughts-become-your-words.

Hung, Melissa. "Meet the 70-Year-Old Runner Who Ran 7 Marathons on 7 Continents in 7 Days." February 22, 2017. https://www.nbcnews.com/news/asian-america/meet-70-year-old-runner-who-ran-7-marathons-7-n722551.

Jammiespree. "The Importance of Mindset." March 3, 2020. Video. 6:01. https://www.youtube.com/watch?v=lJFJfPaYlBs.

Pugmire, Preston. "Mindset is more important than strategy." TEDx. Video, 13:03. February 25, 2019. https://www.youtube.com/watch?v=YiQQ1EWMFHg.

CHAPTER 6: IT TAKES A VILLAGE

AMA. "Athlete Physicians." *Journal of Ethics.* October 2000. https://journalofethics.ama-assn.org/article/athlete-physicians/2000-10.

Coaching Online. "31 Types of Coaching—A Complete List (2022)." Dec 2021. https://www.coaching-online.org/types-of-coaching.

CHAPTER 7: PREPARATION

Bryant, Kobe. "Kobe Bryant quotes: NBA Hall of Famer's most motivational, inspirational words." 2021. https://www.jsonline.com/story/sports/nba/2021/12/16/kobe-bryant-motivational-quotes-nba-lakers/8667478002/.

Gladwell, Malcolm. *Outliers: The Story of Success.* New York, NY: Little, Brown and Company, 2008.

Harnish, Verne. *Scaling Up: How a Few Companies Make It...and Why the Rest Don't (Rockefeller Habits 2.0).* Charleston, SC: ForbesBooks, 2014.

Hastings, Reed. "Sleep is Our Competition." *Fast Company Magazine.* 2017. https://www.fastcompany.com/40491939/netflix-ceo-reed-hastings-sleep-is-our-competition.

McDaniels, Thomas. "3 Timeless Tips That Work Without Fail." 2019. https://thomasmcdaniels.com/3-timeless-tips-that-work-without-fail/.

CHAPTER 8: GRIT

Adams, Robert Dr. *Six Days of Impossible: Nay SEAL Hell Week—A Doctor Looks Back.* Manitoba, Canada: FriesenPress, 2017.

Chi Running. "Learn Better Technique from the Ground up." https://www.chirunning.com/training/technique/.

Duckworth, Angela. *Grit: The Power of Passion and Perseverance.* New York, NY: Simon & Schuster, 2016.

Encyclopedia Britannica. *Salt March | Indian history.* February 2016. http://www.britannica.com/event/Salt-March.

Luttrell, M. *Lone Survivor.* New York, NY: Little, Brown & Company, 2007.

Roosevelt, Eleanor. "Do one thing every day..." RelicsWorld. https://www.relicsworld.com/eleanor-roosevelt/do-one-thing-every-day-that-scares-you-author-eleanor-roosevelt.

Zemeckis, Robert, dir. *Forrest Gump.* Hollywood, CA: Paramount Pictures, 1994.

CHAPTER 9: PROGRESS

Amabile, Teresa M. and Steven Kramer. *The Progress Principle.* Boston, MA: Harvard Business Review Press, 2011.

Macy, Travis. *The Ultra Mindset: An Endurance Champion's 8 Core Principles for Success in Business, Sports, and Life.* Boston: Da Capo Lifelong Books, 2015.

NLP Radio. "The Importance of Progress | NLP | Tony Robbins." April 2021. Video, 4.13. https://www.youtube.com/watch?v=2ue805EREwY.

CHAPTER 10: AUDACITY

Cameron, James, dir. *Titanic.* Hollywood, California: Paramount Pictures, 1997.

Edward, Olivia. "Did the famous Shackleton ad ever run?" Geographical.co.uk. geographical.co.uk/people/explorers/item/339-did-the-famous-shackleton-ad-ever-run.

CHAPTER 11: FINISHING STRONG

Blair, Gary Ryan. "Finish Strong. Glory Awaits." Mind Munchies, Sep 6, 2018. https://medium.com/mind-munchies/make-your-future-bigger-than-your-past-1625dbbb5bc8.

Neil, Connor. "I Can't Focus, How to Learn to Focus." Moving People to Action, January 23, 2017. https://conorneill.com/2017/01/31/i-cant-focus-how-to-learn-to-focus/.

Sharma, Robin (@RobinSharma). "Starting strong is good. Finishing strong is epic." Twitter, June 14, 2017. 6:01 p.m. https://twitter.com/RobinSharma/status/875126183926673409.

Made in the USA
Monee, IL
20 June 2023

35930927R00116